JOURNAL OF BIBLICAL LITERATURE
MONOGRAPH SERIES, VOLUME I

# THE LIVES
# OF THE PROPHETS

Greek Text and Translatic

*by*

## CHARLES CUTLER TORREY

Professor of Semitic Languages, *Emeritus*,
in Yale University

~

*A grant from The Lucius N. Littauer Foundation, has supplied
the funds needed for printing this book.*

SOCIETY OF BIBLICAL LITERATURE AND EXEGESIS
222 NORTH FIFTEENTH STREET
PHILADELPHIA 2, PENNSYLVANIA

1946

# THE LIVES OF THE PROPHETS

Printed in the United States of America
on acid-free paper
∞

FOR some years the Society of Biblical Literature and Exegesis has debated the plan to publish a series of monographs dealing with the results of biblical research. While the need for such a medium for the publication of selected doctoral dissertations and investigations of mature scholars has never been questioned, the obstacles facing such an enterprise seemed insurmountable.

At last a fortunate combination of circumstances has made it possible to launch this Series auspiciously. First of all, its first volume is a work of particular interest, important *per se* because it brings to the attention of biblical scholars an ancient text which has been neglected too long; and important because it is an admirable contribution of an eminent biblical and Semitic scholar, Professor Charles C. Torrey, whose first publication (dealing with Ezra-Nehemiah) was published half a century ago as the second volume of a series similar to ours (Beihefte der Zeitschrift für die alttestamentliche Wissenschaft). In the second place, The Lucius N. Littauer Foundation of New York, through the good offices of its President, Harry Starr, Esq., has generously provided the funds needed for the publication of this volume, thus earning the lasting gratitude of the Society of Biblical Literature and Exegesis.

ROBERT H. PFEIFFER

Editor of the *Journal of Biblical Literature*

# PREFACE

THE ancient Jewish traditions here published have not been as well known as they deserve to be. Eberhard Nestle in his *Marginalien und Materialien*, a work to which constant reference will be made in the following pages, spoke of the neglect of this little collection of legends during "more than a century and a half"; this was in 1893. The half century which has elapsed since that date has seen a most important advance in the scientific study of the *Lives*, a gain which is largely the fruit of Nestle's own labors, but is chiefly embodied in Theodor Schermann's admirable collection and presentation of the extant material. All the hard work preliminary to an edition of the Greek text was thus accomplished.

The original document was not Greek, however, but Semitic. The translation idiom is unmistakable to the expert in Semitics who has gained familiarity with this variety of Greek. The task therefore remained of criticizing the text from the Semitic side, with such occasional use of conjecture as is indispensable in the absence of the original; for no Greek translation is without its errors, which are more or less obvious to the well equipped interpreter.

The original language in this case is easily seen to have been Hebrew, and the recognition of this fact shows the way to that form of the extant Greek which most nearly represents the translator's own achievement.

The document which emerges is a characteristic deposit of old Jewish folklore, first published in Palestine, in the Hebrew language, in the first century of the present era. What is here presented is a Greek text which is believed to be the oldest form now attainable, with such slight emendation as is absolutely necessary, and with the critical and explanatory notes which

[ 1 ]

are required. The appended translation, with its annotations, will probably be welcome; for no English version of these legends has been available.

At all events, with the appearance of the present edition the *Lives* can take its legitimate place, for the first time, as a regular member of the Old Testament Apocrypha.

# INTRODUCTION

THE title, "Lives of the Prophets," by which the work is known could be misleading, for it is by no means a series of biographies, but rather a collection of extra-Biblical Jewish traditions concerning the history and the activities of these famous men. In a few cases the new material may cover two or three pages, while in others two or three sentences will suffice. A uniform pattern is followed throughout, as appears in the superscription which in varying form is prefixed to each of the chief recensions: *"The Names of the Prophets, whence they were, where they died, and how and where they were buried."* In one case at least, that of the prophet Joel, the scheme is followed in the briefest possible terms, with no other word regarding him.

It has therefore sometimes been suggested that the chief interest of the author of this compilation may have been in the localities that are named. Sacred sites are a great asset to any land; the shrines or tombs of saints and heroes have always been venerated. Palestine had good reason to cherish such memorials, and pilgrims to the holy land were eager to seek them out. This motive was present, no doubt, in the author's plan, but it does not appear to have played an important part. The localities are named, and cities and towns are given the coveted honor, in a manner which suggests literary routine rather than the attempt to give useful information. The fragmentary material, so uneven in extent and character, was held together and given unity by this framework of necessary detail.

The main fact to be observed in all these "Lives" is that they are supplementary to the accounts given in the canonical scriptures. Perfect familiarity with the Bible is taken for granted, and there is no intention of repeating what has already been recorded. Jeremiah's career in Jerusalem, for example, is well known, so our compiler turns at once to his activities in Egypt.

[ 3 ]

The wonderful deeds of Daniel in Babylon have no mention; his chapter deals chiefly and at considerable length with the popular notions in regard to the transformation of Nebuchadnezzar. When Jonah's turn comes, the whale and Nineveh are put aside, and his biography is filled out with the traditions concerning his life in the region of Tyre and Sidon with his mother, who entertained Elijah, and with the account of his subsequent journeyings and his burial in the tomb of Othniel. The folk-tales about Habakkuk, Nathan, the dire consequences of the murder of Zechariah ben Jehoiada, etc., also stand quite outside the canonical tradition. Biographies made up from O. T. narratives — and there are such in certain editions of the Lives — are under the suspicion of being a secondary element in the compilation.

Accounts of the Hebrew prophets are a multitude, as would be expected, and this most ancient collection, the Lives, exists in several different recensions. Of these, the most familiar is the one which appears in the works of Epiphanius, Bishop of Salamis in Cyprus (fourth century), and in the earlier time he was very commonly believed to have been its author. The Epiphanius version exists in two distinct forms, the one briefer than the other.

An elaborate edition including much more material than that which is contained in the Lives (which however were kept separate) was falsely attributed to Dorotheus, the learned presbyter of Antioch (late third century and early fourth), who is said to have removed to Tyre; and who was erroneously claimed to have been Bishop of that city. Both Epiphanius and Dorotheus were known to have been familiar with the Hebrew language, and this fact is presumably the reason for the false attributions.

A fourth recension, which proves to be the most important of all, is not attributed to any author, but gives clear evidence of handing down an old tradition. Its chief representative is the text of the Lives contained in one of the principal manuscripts of the Greek Old Testament, the famous Codex Marchalianus, commonly designated by the letter Q. Closely related to this Greek, and usually following it word for word, is the principal Syriac version of the Lives, at least as old as the sixth century.

Recent interest in the Lives is very largely due to the publications of Dr. Eberhard Nestle. In the first edition (1881) of his Syriac Grammar he included in the Chrestomathy the lives of the four Major Prophets, edited from three manuscripts of the British Museum. This proved to be interesting reading for students beginning the study of the Syriac language, and in the second edition of the Grammar (German 1888, English 1889) he added the remaining prophets of the group.

An American scholar, Dr. Isaac H. Hall, became interested in the Lives of the Prophets, and made search for new material in the libraries of New York and Philadelphia. In the *Journal of Biblical Literature*, Vol. 6 (1886), he published an article on "A Hagiologic Manuscript in the Philadelphia Library," and on pages 29–39 printed the Greek text of the portion containing the Lives. This is in the main a very good example of the Q-type of text (see above). In the next number of the same *Journal* (1887), pages 28–40, Hall published "The Lives of the Prophets," containing his translation of this portion of a Syriac manuscript belonging to the library of Union Theological Seminary in New York. This is a version of inferior quality, its text based on that of the Syriac mentioned above, but considerably altered (as though it were a version made from memory). A Berlin ms. has the same text, see Schermann, page 24 . On page 38 Hall expressed himself as "strongly of the opinion" that Syriac was the original language of the Lives, the Greek being a translation (see below).

In Nestle's *Marginalien und Materialien*, Tübingen, 1893, he devoted one section to this subject under the title "Die dem Epiphanius zugeschriebenen *Vitae Prophetarum* in doppelter griechischer Rezension." Here he brought together a mass of valuable notes and references, the collection of many years, and printed on opposite pages the two most important Greek texts of the Lives: on the left that of the manuscript Q (Cod. Vat. 2125), and on the right that of the Paris MS 1115, the chief representative of the Epiphanius recension. He also gave a complete list of the variant readings of the three Syriac mss. of the British Museum. This whole section of his book, pages 1–83, was also published as a separate pamphlet.

Nestle was keenly conscious that he had made only a beginning, and (p. 43) mourned the lack of opportunity to carry the study farther, quoting John 4 37, "One soweth and another reapeth."

The task was taken up and carried through by a very worthy "reaper," Professor Theodor Schermann of the University of Munich, who published in 1907 the results of his work. In Vol. XXXI of the *Texte und Untersuchungen* appeared his Essay, 133 pages, entitled "Die Vitae Prophetarum," a model of thoroughness and clear statement, in which the bewildering mass of material is brought into order and appraised in detail. In the same year he published in the Teubner Series of classical texts a corpus of the Greek and Latin material, the text of each of the several recensions with the variant readings, together with the similar material dealing with the Apostles and Disciples, a volume of 255 pages, with useful Indices (*Prophetarum Vitae Fabulosae*, etc., Lipsiae, 1907).

These two publications are, and will continue to be, indispensable to all students of the Lives. Nevertheless, there is something more to be done. Schermann, like many of his predecessors, pronounced the Lives a Jewish composition. He thought it probably a work of the first century, and postulated a Hebrew original ("hebräische Grundschrift"); see his Essay, pages 119–121, 132. If now it is found to be a worthy member of the Jewish "apocryphal" group, on the same footing as the Testaments of the Twelve Patriarchs, the legends in the first chapters of 2 Maccabees, etc. (*ibid.*, p. IV), there is need of a standard text, to which reference can be made. No one of the recensions thus far published can be thought acceptable as it stands; all are seen to be corrupt in greater or less degree, and the choice among them, in the need of a single homogeneous manuscript tradition that could be treated as authoritative, has not been found easy. And every member of the group has its occasional readings which are too absurd to be tolerated.

The names of places, obviously Greek transliterations of Semitic, are in much need of correction from the Hebrew side. The ridiculous "Behemoth" in the Life of Daniel, attested directly or indirectly in every form of the narrative, appears at its worst (as "the God of Israel") in Schermann's A-text. In this

[ 6 ]

text also is found the information that the prophet Nathan, of Gibeon (near Jerusalem) was "of the tribe of Thōi." Everybody knew that there was no such Hebrew tribe. In the Life of Jeremiah we read of reptiles "which the Egyptians call *ephōth* (vipers) and the Greeks call crocodiles." Jonah was buried in the tomb of Othniel, "who was the Judge of one tribe" (!). All these blunders and numerous others, can be explained and corrected as translations from Hebrew, but in no other way. It is because of the number of these disturbing readings, beyond much doubt, that the little document has been given such slight attention.

It has generally been taken for granted that Greek was the original language of the book, but two exceptions are recorded. Joachim Zehner, whose work was published at Schleusingen in 1612, attempted to show that the original was Hebrew, but his conclusions seem to have met with little favor (Nestle, *Marg.*, p. 2). The other advocate of the theory of translation was a Dutch scholar, H. A. Hamaker, author of a *Commentatio in libellum de vita et morte prophetarum*, Amsterdam, 1833. His work failed to convince either Nestle or Schermann; and the few specimens of his criticism which the latter records usually are not such as to inspire confidence; one exception, however, will be mentioned below. Schermann himself, in spite of his postulate of a "hebräische Grundschrift," would entertain no theory of translation, but believed the work to have been composed in a sort of Jewish-Greek *patois* (Vitae Prophetarum, p. 122). This opinion, it is hardly necessary to say, was held also by Nestle. In the following pages it will appear that the original language was Hebrew, and the Greek a translation.

Thanks to the recognizable *errors* in Hebrew archetype or Greek interpretation, and the very definite information which they give as to the original wording of the translation, the problem of the oldest form of the existing Greek is simplified. It becomes possible to point out the most reliable witness, and indeed to reach the conclusion that we possess almost unchanged what the author of the Lives wrote. It will be shown that all the known texts of this collection of traditions relating to the Hebrew Prophets are derived directly or indirectly from the version

[ 7 ]

which lies before us in the Q manuscript. There is thus additional ground for the preference which our two chief authorities have already expressed, Nestle emphasizing especially the great age of this text (*Marg.*, 16–18), and Schermann its relative freedom from the slight expansions, embellishments, and Christian interpolations which are more or less in evidence in all the witnesess (*Vitae*, 46).

The list of the prophets who are included in the Lives is not everywhere the same. The three Major Prophets and Daniel and the twelve Minor Prophets form in every complete recension the nucleus, to which occasional additions are made. One list will begin with Moses, Samuel, and David; another, of Christian origin, will end with Zechariah (Luke 1 5 ff.), Simeon (Luke 2 25 ff.), and John the Baptist. The Hebrew list of purely Jewish origin appears to have included Nathan, Ahijah the Shilonite (I Ki, chap. 14), Joed (the prophet of I Ki 13 1–10), Zechariah son of Jehoiada (II Chron 24 20–22), Azariah son of Oded (II Chron, chap. 15), probably also brief notices of Elijah and Elisha (see below). The order of the names in the list varies to some extent. In Greek mss. the order of the LXX would naturally be preferred. A concise account of the variations is given by Schermann, pages 39–42. The order in the present edition, in general that of the Hebrew Bible, is the one followed in Cod. Q, in the Syriac mss., and in the older Epiphanius recension. Beyond doubt, it was the order of the original (Hebrew) edition.

It was remarked, above, that these legends of the prophets are supplementary to the accounts given in the Old Testament. A conspicuous exception seems to be encountered in the biographies of Elijah and Elisha. In both cases, what we see before us is a short paragraph containing details not found in the canonical scriptures, followed by an extended summary of the narratives contained in the books of Kings. These two summaries, moreover, are distinctly marked off by their language, for the Greek is *not* of the translation variety, but is freely composed. The conclusion is certain, that the two expansions are improvements subsequently made in the Greek version, and they are omitted in the present edition. It is interesting to see that they are bracketed by Schermann on the ground of their later attestation (*Vitae*, pages 109–114).

Christian expansions, as would be expected, are to be found here and there in the Lives. Since the prophets were believed to be clairvoyant, and entrusted with the duty of foretelling (in veiled manner) events of especial importance of the history of Israel, it was inevitable that Christian scribes should now and then insert passages to show that this or that prophet had predicted the coming of Jesus the Messiah. Clement *ad Corinthios*, XVII, pictures the Hebrew patriarchs and prophets as "wandering about in sheepskins and goatskins" (Heb 11 37) κηρύσσοντες τὴν ἔλευσιν τοῦ Χριστοῦ, and we see the prediction in this simplest form ascribed to Habakkuk, Malachi, and Azariah ben Oded, in the principal Epiphanius recension.

In the oldest and most reliable text of the Lives there is one place only where the work of a Christian hand is seen, namely in the Life of Jeremiah, and an interesting problem is presented. The prophet tells the priests of Egypt that their sculptured gods will fall, when a virgin with her babe "of divine appearance" shall arrive in Egypt; and the narrator adds, that "to this day" the people of Egypt honor a virgin mother and bow down to a babe which they put in a manger. A few lines farther on, where it is told how Jeremiah deposited the ark of the covenant in a cave which he sealed up, to await the coming of the Lord (II Macc 2 5 ff.), the prophet is made to say: "This shall be for you the sign of his appearance, when all the nations worship a piece of wood" (that is, the cross).

Now it is certain that the author of the Lives was not a Jewish Christian; if he had been, the work would have presented a very different appearance. On the other hand, it will not do to detach the long passage relating to the Virgin Mary and her child, treating it as a later addition. It does not at all have the appearance of an interpolation; in particular, the passage relating to Ptolemy and his inquiry is plainly Egyptian folklore, not the invention of an interpolator. Though written by a Christian, it belongs to the original text of the Lives.

The solution of the problem may perhaps be seen in the peculiar history of this one of all the Hebrew prophets and in the traditions relating to him. The Jeremiah folklore of this early time is largely Egyptian, the rabbinical legends come from a later day. The stories of his career after fleeing from Jerusalem are handed down in the "Biblical" literature of several languages current in the region of the Nile, Greek, Ethiopic, Coptic, and Arabic.

The author of the Lives appears to have been a man of Jerusalem (see below), but his story of Jeremiah was told, or written, by an Egyptian. In the second paragraph the man from Egypt (who presumably was resident in Jerusalem) names his authorities — a most unusual happening: "We have been told by the children of Antigonus and Ptolemy, aged men," etc. Tradition of this quality was not to be set aside, and the Christian element could be recorded for whatever it might be worth.

Equally Egyptian is all the remaining portion of the narrative, based on the Aramaic Letter which "the men of Jerusalem and Judea and the senate of the Jews" sent in the year 124 B. C. to Aristobulus and the Jewish leaders in Egypt (II Macc 1 10–2 18).

The textual history of the portion of the Life which deals with the reptiles of Egypt presents so many unusual features that it has seemed best to reserve it for separate treatment. See the Appendix, below.

Aside from the Jeremiah chapter, the little book is Palestinian through and through, and its atmosphere is distinctly that of pre-Christian times. Very noticeable is the number of geographical names, familiar to the author and his contemporaries but unknown to us and unmentioned in either the early Christian Onomastica or the rabbinical writings, which occur in the Lives. Such are "Sarīra" (home of Ezekiel), "Beth-hakkerem" (Obadiah), "Kiryath-maōn" (Jonah), "Sabaratha" (Zephaniah), "Sōphā" (Malachi), and "Sūbatha" (Azariah ben Oded). It is generally impossible to make even a probable guess as to the original form of the name, or as to the location. "Deborah's oak" near Bethel, mentioned in the life of Jonah, is known from the Old Testament, but "the oak of Shiloh," twice mentioned here, is otherwise unknown.

In the life of Isaiah the Greek text presents an "oak of Rogel," δρῦς ʿΡωγήλ, which is neither heard of elsewhere nor quite plausible here. The phrase has been allowed to stand in the Greek, but in the Translation it is corrected to "fountain of Rogel." The name of the celebrated spring is elsewhere invariably 'Ēn-rogel, and the conjecture of the Dutch scholar H. A. Hamaker (see above) that in the original Hebrew text the word 'ēn, "spring," was mistaken for 'ēṣ, "tree," the two words being practically identical in the Hebrew script, seems the true explanation of the anomaly. The Greek δρῦς has the same general meaning, "tree," as the Hebrew word.

The standpoint of the author of the Lives is plainly Jerusalem. In the life of Zephaniah, and also in that of Daniel, "the city" is Zion. The fact seems to appear with especial clearness in the life of Nahum, where the location (otherwise unknown) of the Prophet's city, Elkosh, is given: "beyond" (*something*; for a noun has been lost from the Greek text) "in the direction of Beth-gabrīn." Whether the precarious guess, "mountains," is right or wrong, the standpoint of the writer can hardly be any other than Jerusalem. It is tempting to connect Elqōš with the city-ruin Umm-Lāqis (Buhl, *Geographie des alten Palästina*, 191; Robinson, *Biblical Researches* [1841], II, 388), since the location is exactly what is required.

The dating of the Lives in the first century of the present era will hardly be questioned by any one who examines the evidence presented here. It was remarked, above, that this date was preferred by Schermann, on the sole basis of the Greek evidence. The probability is very strong, moreover, that the work was composed and given out before the year 80; the time, approximately, when the anathema was issued by Gamaliel II against the Christians and their writings. The Jewish author would have been far less likely, after that date, to adopt for the story of the prophet Jeremiah the tradition — whatever its interest — furnished by the Jewish-Christian narrator from Egypt (see above).

There is other evidence to be taken into account. We learn from the Life of Elijah that at the time when this work was composed Gilead was, and for some time had been, a part of the Nabatean kingdom. This "Arabian" territory, as we know, had included even the city of Damascus, and the testimony of the

[ 11 ]

apostle Paul to a time shortly before the year 40 is familiar
(II Cor 11 32). Damascus was taken over by the Romans about
the year 63, however, and remained in their hands, but the
adjoining territory continued to be Nabatean. In the year 67,
the king Maliku contributed troops to the army of Vespasian
for the Jewish war (Josephus, *War*, 3, iv, 2); certainly at that
time Gilead was "Arabian." The reign of Maliku ended in 71,
and his successor, Rabel, is the last Nabatean king of whom
we have certain knowledge. This Arabia became a Roman
province in the year 106. See Schürer, *Geschichte³*, I, 737 ff.

From these facts nothing more definite can be gained for our
purpose, but the evidence that the book of the *Lives* was composed in the first century, not later, is confirmed from a new
side. The time indicated by the allusion to the Nabateans, in the
Life of Elijah, would then be either the closing years of the reign
of Maliku or the early years of Rabel, if the probability claimed
above is agreed to. As for the story of the virgin and child in
Egypt, the present writer has already presented evidence in
some variety to show that the Gospel of Matthew was published
not later than the year 50.

To gain a Greek text which shall be both readable and authoritative (for no text hitherto published has satisfied either of these
requirements) it is necessary to make Q the basis, and to criticize
its readings with the aid of (1) a small and select apparatus,
and (2) recognition of the underlying Hebrew. The need of
emendation by conjecture is imperative, as it is in all Greek
translations from Semitic documents which have perished.

The text of Q, as it stands before us, represents a secondary
stage in the manuscript transmission, for it has experienced some
alteration and expansion; on the other hand, the evidence is
clear and gratifying that as here emended it stands very near
to the text of the original Greek translation. Underlying all
the numerous and varied manuscript witnesses that have been
preserved and that Schermann has so carefully edited, there is
a single stable tradition that can be recognized; no one of the
principal witnesses has altered it notably, and the fact has
already been stated that Q is decidedly its best representative.

For a concise description of this 6th-century manuscript see

[ 12 ]

Swete's *Introduction to the Old Testament in Greek*, 144 f. The prefixed leaves containing the Lives of the Prophets may be of the same century as the rest, though written by a later hand, and their text may, of course, have been copied from a much older manuscript. The actual reading which they give has already been published in Nestle's *Marginalien*, and in Schermann's *recensio anonyma*, pp. 68–98 of his Teubner edition.

The critical apparatus here used in preparing the text is a meager selection in point of numbers, but it probably will be found adequate for its purpose. There was but one Greek translation of the Lives, and all the known texts are derived from it. The several types of the Greek which are to be compared are the following:

1. The principal "Epiphanius" recension, already mentioned; the text obtained from MS. 1115 of the Bibliothèque Nationale, published in Nestle's *Marginalien*, and in Schermann's text edition, pp. 8–25. This is an expanded and embellished edition, in which some of the chief difficulties have been smoothed over. It is the version of the Lives which has been most familiar.

2. A briefer form of the work, also attributed to Epiphanius. This includes the Major and Minor Prophets, somewhat expanded accounts of Elijah and Elisha, and the life of Zechariah ben Jehoiada, mistakenly appended to the life of Zechariah ben Berechiah, as its second half. The text is generally good, and indeed to be preferred to that of the recension just described, but is very often abbreviated. Schermann edits it from seven manuscripts, pp. 55–67.

3. The "Dorotheus" recension. In this, in the lives of the writing prophets and Elijah, the account of each prophet consists of two divisions, the former estimating the man and his work from the Christian point of view, the latter giving the original Jewish version. This latter text, because of its simplicity and its freedom from Christian influence (except in the case of Jeremiah!), Schermann was inclined to regard as the oldest of our witnesses. It is clearly derived from the text of Q, however, as will be seen. Schermann edits from several Greek sources, and gives many Latin variant readings. A Greek witness which he overlooked is the Neapolitan Synopsis, published by Lagarde

in his *Septuaginta Studien*, II (1892), pp. 64–102. In the sections containing the standard Lives, it differs but slightly from the other Dorotheus texts.

The "Scholienrecension" of the lives of the twelve Minor Prophets, contained in the Munich manuscript 472, described by Schermann, pages 19–21, and published in his text-edition, pages 98–104, is both old and interesting, but need not be included in the critical apparatus of this edition, for it can contribute nothing of consequence.

The Syriac version of the Lives appears in numerous forms, which are so fully described by Schermann in his essay, pages 24–39, that there is little to add. All the known Syriac texts appear to be based on a single translation made from the Greek. The best representative is, and will continue to be, the text of the edition from three manuscripts published by Nestle in his Syriac grammar (see above), the best single witness being Brit. Mus. Add. 14,536, a manuscript of the eighth century. This agrees closely with the Greek of Q, and it is clear that the original Syriac translation was made from a text nearly but not quite identical with it.

Regarding the date of the version, there is little that can be said. It is at least as old as the sixth century, this much can be learned from the comparison of its text with that of the Lives of nine of the Minor Prophets contained in the Syro-Hexaplar manuscript (Nestle, pages 8 below, 46 mid.; Schermann, pages 37 f.). The text of these Syriac Lives has not yet been given a separate publication, and it is not very important that this should be done. Nestle and Schermann were mistaken in supposing that this Syriac text is a new translation from a Greek original (like the rest of the Hexaplar Syriac). The evidence is clear that it is merely another form, later and generally inferior, of the version contained in three manuscripts of the British Museum. There was but one Syriac translation, made at an early date, and in the course of centuries it has often been somewhat carelessly copied as well as improved here and there from Greek sources. Certainly there were no corresponding Lives in the Greek Hexapla.

The reason why the redactor of the Codex Ambrosianus left

his task unfinished, failing to include the Lives of Haggai, Zechariah, and Malachi, can only be conjectured. One guess might be, that upon finishing the book of Haggai he passed on at once (very naturally) to the book of the brother-prophet Zechariah, before noticing that he had failed to insert the few lines of biography. Having made this omission, he could hardly do better than to omit likewise the two remaining Lives.

An almost complete Syriac text of the *Lives* is preserved in the important Chronicle of Michael the Syrian, Jacobite Patriarch of Antioch in 1166–1199, which was published in four volumes by J.-B. Chabot in 1899–1910; see Schermann, pages 25 ff. The Lives are scattered about in pages 38–63 of Volume IV, which contains the Syriac text. Schermann included in the footnotes to his edition of the principal Epiphanius recension the readings of Chabot's French translation, contained in Volume I, pages 63–101. It has been found unnecessary to include this Syriac text in the present critical apparatus, for it contains nothing new.

In this manuscript, as in all the others which contain the Syriac Lives, they are attributed to Epiphanius of Cyprus, but this does not imply any connection with the recensions above described. The true association is with the oldest form of the Greek and with the Syriac which follows it so closely. The too hasty guess of Dr. I. H. Hall, already mentioned, that the Greek of the Lives is a rendering from Syriac, rests on no evidence and is easily proved false. It was given undue weight by his successors, who in more than one place have left room for Hall's original Syriac.

In general, it will be found fruitless to attempt to add to the witnesses which have been assembled and classified by Nestle and Schermann. They have done all the main work, and for the present task which remained to be done it was only necessary to rest on what they had achieved.

The relative excellence of the Q-text will appear with sufficient clearness when the notes appended to the present edition are studied. It will perhaps not be superfluous, however, to show in advance, by a few examples, the secondary character of the principal Epiphanius text, which has been the best known and the most usable of all the versions.

[ 15 ]

*Notes 8 and 9.* The passage relating to the *argols* (see the Appendix), in which a transliteration from Hebrew is in evidence. The Ep. recension simply omits bodily the troublesome passage.

*Note 28.* This brings into view the original wording of the Greek translation and of the Hebrew text which it rendered. In the account of the repentance of Nebuchadnezzar in his lucid hours, and of the change from human consciousness to the mind of a dumb animal, it is said in the Greek: "He wept and begged the Lord, praying every day and night forty times. *Behemoth* came upon him, and he forgot that he had been a human being." Ep. expands this nonsense in a most interesting manner.

*Note 31.* The curious reading of Ep. appears to be derived directly from the slightly corrupt text of Cod. Q.

*Note 39.* It can hardly be doubted that the city Beth-meon is the one intended. This is accordingly another instance similar to the preceding. See note 39 on the Translation.

*Note 44.* Ep. not only adopts the foolish identification of Jonah with the child raised to life by Elijah, but also rearranges the whole story.

*Note 47.* The impossible reading obtained from a corrupt Hebrew text of the *Lives* is omitted by Ep.; compare Notes 8 and 9, above.

*Note 72.* One of several cases in which the form of a proper name in Ep. is manifestly later than in the other recensions.

On the other hand, there is one passage in which Ep. alone has preserved the true text; see note 65 on the Greek text, and note 66 on the translation. In the Hebrew text stood חוי; the Greek transliterated, quite regularly, $E\Omega H$; the first copyist wrote $\Theta\Omega H$, with the very frequent confusion of the two letters. If it were not for the unique manuscript, Paris 1115, we should have no record of the highly interesting Hebrew tradition that the prophet Nathan, who taught David the law of Moses, was a Hivite! Since every scribe or reader knew that there was no Hebrew tribe ($\phi v\lambda\acute\eta$) named *Thōi*, the phrase was all but universally omitted.

Other cases in which the Greek interpreter transliterated his Hebrew are the following: $\alpha\rho\gamma o\lambda\alpha$ and $\epsilon\phi\omega\theta$ (see the Appendix), $\beta\epsilon\eta\mu\omega\theta$, $Ev\alpha\kappa\epsilon\iota\mu$ ("Anakim," the legendary giants, whose

[ 16 ]

tombs were to be seen in the neighborhood of Micah's home), Ναουρ, miswritten as Μαουρ (Nahor, the ancestor of Abraham), σφαρσωφτιμ, the title of the book of Judges; also, of course, the names of cities and towns. It is to be observed that these are not in any case transliterations obtained from the Greek Bible, but are the independent work of the translator of the *Lives*.

There is some evidence that in the Hebrew text the vowel-letters *waw* and *yod* were sparingly used. The name of the land of Edom, Se'îr, was written with only three letters, otherwise it would not have appeared in the Greek as Saar (note 45). The name of Elkōsh, the home of Nahum, was not written with a long vowel in the final syllable — and indeed, there is room for doubt as to the true vocalization, see above.

An apparent mistranslation in the Life of Jonah, where Othniel is said to have been "the judge of one tribe," is the result of a false reading in the Hebrew text, the nature of which is readily seen, see note 47. In general, the Hebrew appears to have been well written, and the translation to have been skilfully made.

In editing the Greek text, it has not been thought necessary to record itacisms; and in giving the variants of the Syriac version, a few readings too remote from the Greek tradition to be useful have been omitted.

In the critical notes, MS denotes readings of the Codex Marchalianus (Cod. Vat. 2125), generally known as Q; E represents the longer Epiphanius recension, found in the Paris Ms. 1115; E1, the briefer recension, found in a number of manuscripts; D, the text of the Dorotheus version; Syr., the reading of the Syriac text published in the second edition of Nestle's *Syriac Grammar*.

Ὀνόματα προφητῶν καὶ πόθεν
εἰσὶ καὶ ποῦ ἀπέθανον καὶ
πῶς καὶ ποῦ κεῖνται

# Ἡσαΐας

1   ἦν[1] ἀπὸ Ἰερουσαλήμ. θνῄσκει ὑπὸ Μανασσῆ πρισθεὶς εἰς
    δύο καὶ ἐτέθη ὑποκάτω δρυὸς Ῥωγὴλ ἐχόμενα τῆς διαβάσεως
2   τῶν ὑδάτων ὧν ἀπώλεσεν Ἐζεκίας χώσας αὐτά. καὶ ὁ θεὸς
    τὸ σημεῖον τοῦ Σιλωὰμ διὰ τὸν προφήτην ἐποίησεν· ὅτι πρὸ
    τοῦ θανεῖν ὀλιγωρήσας ηὔξατο πιεῖν ὕδωρ καὶ εὐθέως ἀπεστάλη
    αὐτῷ ἐξ αὐτοῦ· διὰ τοῦτο ἐκλήθη Σιλωάμ, ὃ ἑρμηνεύεται
    ἀπεσταλμένος.
3   Καὶ ἐπὶ τοῦ Ἐζεκία, πρὸ τοῦ ποιῆσαι τοὺς λάκκους καὶ
    τὰς κολυμβήθρας, ἐπὶ εὐχῇ τοῦ Ἡσαΐου μικρὸν ὕδωρ ἐξελή-
    λυθεν, ὅτι ἦν ὁ λαὸς ἐν συγκλεισμῷ ἀλλοφύλων καὶ ἵνα μὴ
4   διφθαρῇ ἡ πόλις ὡς μὴ[2] ἔχουσα ὕδωρ. ἠρώτων γὰρ οἱ
    πολέμιοι, πόθεν πίννουσιν, καὶ ἔχοντες τὴν πόλιν παρεκαθέζοντο
    τῷ Σιλωάμ. ἐὰν οὖν οἱ Ἰουδαῖοι ἤρχοντο, ἐξήρχετο ὕδωρ· ἐὰν
    δὲ ἀλλόφυλοι, οὔ. διὸ ἕως σήμερον αἰφνιδίως ἐξέρχεται, ἵνα
5   δειχθῇ τὸ μυστήριον. καὶ ἐπειδὴ διὰ τοῦ Ἡσαΐου τοῦτο γέγονεν,
    μνήμης χάριν καὶ ὁ λαὸς πλησίον αὐτὸν ἐπιμελῶς ἔθαψεν καὶ
    ἐνδόξως, ἵνα διὰ εὐχῶν αὐτοῦ καὶ μετὰ θάνατον αὐτοῦ ὡσαύτως
    ἔχωσι τὴν ἀπόλαυσιν τοῦ ὕδατος, ὅτι καὶ χρησμὸς ἐδόθη αὐτοῖς
    περὶ αὐτοῦ.
6   Ἔστι δὲ ὁ τάφος ἐχόμενα τοῦ τάφου τῶν βασιλέων ὄπισθεν
7   τοῦ τάφου τῶν ἱερέων ἐπὶ τὸ μέρος τὸ πρὸς νότον. Σαλωμὼν
    γὰρ ἐποίησε τοὺς τάφους, τοῦ Δαυὶδ διαγράψαντος, κατ'
    ἀνατολὰς τῆς Σιών, ἥτις ἔχει εἴσοδον ἀπὸ Γαβαὼν μήκοθεν τῆς
    πόλεως σταδίοις εἴκοσι, καὶ ἐποίησε σκολιὰν σύνθεσιν ἀνυ-
    πονόητον· καὶ ἔστιν ἕως τῆς σήμερον τοῖς πολλοῖς *τῶν ἱερέων[3]
8   ἀγνοουμένη, ὅλου δὲ τοῦ λαοῦ. ἐκεῖ εἶχεν ὁ βασιλεὺς τὸ χρυσίον
9   τὸ ἐξ Αἰθιοπίας καὶ τὰ ἀρώματα. καὶ ἐπειδὴ ὁ Ἐζεκίας ἔδειξεν
    τοῖς ἔθνεσι τὸ μυστήριον Δαυὶδ καὶ Σαλωμῶνος καὶ ἐμίανεν

---

[1] MS om.
[2] MS om.
[3] Inserted from D and Syr.

ὀστᾶ[4] πατέρων αὐτοῦ, διὰ τοῦτο ὁ θεὸς ἐπηράσατο εἰς δου-
λείαν ἔσεσθαι τὸ σπέρμα αὐτοῦ τοῖς ἐχθροῖς αὐτοῦ, καὶ
ἄκαρπον αὐτὸν ἐποίησεν ὁ θεὸς ἀπὸ τῆς ἡμέρας ἐκείνης.

## Ἰ ε ρ ε μ ί α ς

1 ἦν ἐξ Ἀναθὼθ καὶ ἐν Τάφναις Αἰγύπτου λίθοις βληθεὶς ὑπὸ
2 τοῦ λαοῦ ἀποθνήσκει. κεῖται δὲ ἐν τῷ τόπῳ τῆς οἰκήσεως
Φαραώ, ὅτι οἱ Αἰγύπτιοι ἐδόξασαν αὐτὸν εὐεργετηθέντες δι'
3 αὐτοῦ. ηὔξατο γὰρ καὶ αἱ ἀσπίδες αὐτοὺς ἔασαν,[5] [ἃς] καλοῦσιν
4 οἱ Αἰγύπτιοι ἐφώθ. καὶ ὅσοι εἰσὶ πιστοὶ θεοῦ ἕως σήμερον
εὔχονται ἐν τῷ τόπῳ καὶ λαμβάνοντες τοῦ χοὸς τοῦ τόπου
5 δήγματα ἀσπίδων θεραπεύουσι.[6] ἡμεῖς δὲ ἠκούσαμεν ἐκ τῶν
παίδων Ἀντιγόνου καὶ Ρτολεμαίου γερόντων ἀνδρῶν, ὅτι
Ἀλέξανδρος ὁ Μακεδὼν ἐπιστὰς τῷ τόπῳ τοῦ προφήτου καὶ
ἐπιγνοὺς αὐτοῦ τὰ μυστήρια εἰς Ἀλεξάνδρειαν μετέστησεν
6 αὐτοῦ τὰ λείψανα, περιθεὶς αὐτὰ ἐνδόξως κύκλῳ· καὶ ἐκωλύθη
ἐκ τῆς γῆς τὸ γένος τῶν ἀσπίδων,[7] καὶ οὕτως ἐνέβαλεν *τοὺς
ὄφεις[8] τοὺς λεγομένους ἀργόλας, ὅ ἐστιν ὀφιομάχους.[9]
7 Οὗτος ὁ Ἰερεμίας σημεῖον δέδωκε τοῖς ἱερεῦσιν Αἰγύπτου,
ὅτι δεῖ σεισθῆναι τὰ εἴδωλα αὐτῶν καὶ συμπεσεῖν τὰ χειροποί-
ητα πάντα ὅταν ἐπιβῇ ἐν Αἰγύπτῳ παρθένος λοχεύουσα σὺν
8 βρέφει θεοειδεῖ. δι' ὃ καὶ ἕως νῦν τιμῶσι παρθένον λοχὸν καὶ
βρέφος ἐν φάτνῃ τιθέντες προσκυνοῦσι, καὶ Πτολεμαίῳ τῷ βα-
σιλεῖ τὴν αἰτίαν πυνθανομένῳ ἔλεγον, ὅτι πατροπαράδοτόν ἐστι

---

4 MS+τόπου, perhaps originating in the τα preceding and the πα following.
5 MS continues: καὶ τῶν ὑδάτων οἱ θῆρες οὓς καλοῦσιν οἱ Αἰγύπτιοι μὲν
νεφώθ, Ἕλληνες δὲ κροκοδείλους. Thus also the other witnesses, D and
E1 reading ἐφώθ. But the crocodiles are plainly a later addition.
6 All the texts add (with slight variations) καὶ πολλοὶ αὐτὰ τὰ θηρία (καὶ)
τὰ τοῦ ὕδατος φυγαδεύουσιν.
7 All texts add καὶ ἐκ τοῦ ποταμοῦ ὡσαύτως τοὺς κροκοδείλους.
8 MS, D, and Syr. insert here τοὺς ὄφεις (E and E1 omit the whole passage). See the Appendix.
9 Grk. inserts an etymological note concerning the argols, οὓς ἤνεγκεν ἐκ
τοῦ Ἄργους τῆς Πελοποννήσου, ὅθεν καὶ ἀργόλαι καλοῦνται, τοῦτ' ἔστιν
Ἄργους δεξιοί. λαιὰν γὰρ λέγουσι πᾶν εὐώνυμον.

μυστήριον ὑπὸ ὁσίου προφήτου, τοῖς πατράσιν ἡμῶν παρα-
δοθέν, καὶ ἐκδεχόμεθα τὸ πέρας, φησίν, τοῦ μυστηρίου αὐτοῦ.¹⁰

9   Οὗτος ὁ προφήτης πρὸ τῆς ἁλώσεως τοῦ ναοῦ ἥρπαξε τὴν
κιβωτὸν τοῦ νόμου καὶ τὰ ἐν αὐτῇ¹¹ καὶ ἐποίησεν αὐτὰ καταπο-
10 θῆναι ἐν πέτρᾳ, καὶ εἶπε τοῖς παρεστῶσιν· Ἀπεδήμησεν κύριος
ἐκ Σινᾶ¹² εἰς οὐρανὸν καὶ πάλιν ἐλεύσεται ἐν δυνάμει, καὶ
σημεῖον ὑμῖν ἔσται τῆς παρουσίας αὐτοῦ, ὅτε ξύλον πάντα τὰ
11 ἔθνη προσκυνοῦσιν. εἶπεν δὲ ὅτι τὴν κιβωτὸν ταύτην οὐδεὶς ἐκ-
βάλλει εἰ μὴ Ἀαρών, καὶ τὰς ἐν αὐτῷ πλάκας οὐδεὶς ἀναπτύξει
οὐκέτι ἱερέων ἢ προφητῶν εἰ μὴ Μωϋσῆς ὁ ἐκλεκτὸς τοῦ θεοῦ.
12 καὶ ἐν τῇ ἀναστάσει πρώτῃ ἡ κιβωτὸς ἀναστήσεται καὶ ἐξελεύ-
σεται ἐκ τῆς πέτρας καὶ τεθήσεται ἐν ὄρει Σινᾶ, καὶ πάντες οἱ
ἅγιοι πρὸς αὐτὴν¹³ συναχθήσονται ἐκεῖ ἐκδεχόμενοι κύριον καὶ
τὸν ἐχθρὸν φεύγοντες ἀνελεῖν αὐτοὺς θέλοντα.
13   Ἐν τῇ πέτρᾳ ἐσφράγισε τῷ δακτύλῳ τὸ ὄνομα τοῦ θεοῦ καὶ
γέγονεν ὁ τύπος ὡς γλυφὴ σιδήρου, καὶ νεφέλη ἐσκέπασε τὸ
ὄνομα καὶ οὐδεὶς νοεῖ τὸν τόπον οὔτε ἀναγνῶναι αὐτὸν¹⁴ ἕως
14 σήμερον καὶ ἕως συντελείας.¹⁵ καὶ ἔστιν ἡ πέτρα ἐν τῇ ἐρήμῳ,
ὅπου πρώτως ἡ κιβωτὸς γέγονε μεταξὺ τῶν δύο ὀρέων, ἐν οἷς
κεῖνται Μωϋσῆς καὶ Ἀαρών, καὶ ἐν νυκτὶ νεφέλη ὡς πῦρ γίνεται
κατὰ τὸν τύπον τὸν ἀρχαῖον, ὅτι οὐ μὴ παύσηται ἡ δόξα τοῦ
15 θεοῦ ἐκ τοῦ νόμου αὐτοῦ. καὶ ἔδωκεν ὁ θεὸς τῷ Ἰερεμίᾳ χάριν,
ἵνα τὸ τέλος τοῦ μυστηρίου αὐτοῦ αὐτὸς ποιήσειεν, ἵνα γένηται
συνκοινωνὸς Μωϋσέως, καὶ ὁμοῦ εἰσὶν ἕως σήμερον.


## Ἰεζεκιήλ

1   Οὗτός ἐστιν ἐκ γῆς Σαρίρα,¹⁶ ἐκ τῶν ἱερέων, καὶ ἀπέθανεν
ἐν τῇ γῇ τῶν Χαλδαίων¹⁷ ἐπὶ τῆς αἰχμαλωσίας, πολλὰ προφη-
2 τεύσας τοῖς ἐν τῇ Ἰουδαίᾳ. ἀπέκτεινε δὲ αὐτὸν ὁ ἡγούμενος τοῦ

---

¹⁰ Regarding this passage, which has the appearance of a Christian interpolation, see the Introduction.
¹¹ MS αὐτῷ.           ¹² MS Σιών.         ¹³ MS αὐτόν.
¹⁴ Some Grk. mss. add δύναται or δυνήσεται, but the Heb. idiom requires
no verb.
¹⁵ Ἕως συντελείας is Heb. 'ad kallēh, II Ki. 13 17, 19; Ezra 9 14.
¹⁶ MS Ἀρίρα, Syr. Sarīda.
¹⁷ Τῶν Χαλδαίων renders Kasdīm, probably here as often the name of the
country, "Chaldea."

λαοῦ Ἰσραὴλ ἐκεῖ, ἐλεγχόμενος ὑπ' αὐτοῦ ἐπὶ εἰδώλων σεβάσ-
3  μασι. καὶ ἔθαψαν αὐτὸν ἐν ἀγρῷ Μαοὺρ[18] ἐν τάφῳ Σὴμ καὶ
4  Ἀρφάξαδ πατέρων Ἀβραάμ. καὶ ἔστιν ὁ τάφος σπήλαιον
   διπλοῦν, ὅτι[19] καὶ Ἀβραὰμ ἐν Χεβρῶν πρὸς τὴν ὁμοιότητα
5  αὐτοῦ ἐποίησε τὸν τάφον Σάρρας. διπλοῦν δὲ λέγεται, ὅτι
   εἰλικτόν ἐστι, καὶ ἀπόκρυφον ἐξ ἐπιπέδου ὑπερῷον[20] ἐστι ἐπὶ
   γῆς ἐν πέτρᾳ κρεμάμενον.
6  Οὗτος ὁ προφήτης τέρας ἔδωκε τῷ λαῷ, ὥστε[21] προσέχειν
7  τῷ ποταμῷ Χοβάρ· ὅτε ἐκλείποι, ἐπελπίζειν τὸ δρέπανον τῆς
   ἐρημώσεως εἰς πέρας τῆς γῆς, καὶ ὅτε πλημμυρήσῃ, τὴν εἰς
8  Ἱερουσαλὴμ ἐπάνοδον. καὶ γὰρ ἐκεῖ κατῴκει ὁ ὅσιος καὶ πολλοὶ
9  πρὸς αὐτὸν συνεστρέφοντο. καὶ ποτὲ πλήθους συνόντος αυτῷ
   ἔδεισαν οἱ Χαλδαῖοι, μὴ ἀντάρωσι, καὶ ἐπῆλθον αὐτοῖς εἰς
10 ἀναίρεσιν. καὶ ἐποίησεν στῆναι τὸ ὕδωρ, ἵνα ἐκφύγωσιν εἰς
   τὸ πέραν γενόμενοι· καὶ οἱ τολμήσαντες τῶν ἐχθρῶν ἐπιδιῶξαι
   κατεποντίσθησαν.
11 Οὗτος διὰ προσευχῆς αὐτομάτως αὐτοῖς δαψιλῆ τροφὴν
   ἰχθύων παρέσχετο καὶ πολλοῖς ἐκλείπουσι ζωὴν ἐλθεῖν ἐκ θεοῦ
   παρεκάλεσεν.
12 Οὗτος ἀπολλυμένου τοῦ λαοῦ ὑπὸ τῶν ἐχθρῶν προσῆλθε τοῖς
13 ἡγουμένοις καὶ διὰ τεραστίων φοβηθέντες ἐπαύσαντο. τοῦτό τε
   ἔλεγεν αὐτοῖς, ὅτι Διαπεφωνήκαμεν; ἀπώλετο ἡ ἐλπὶς ἡμῶν;
   καὶ ἐν τέρατι τῶν ὀστέων τῶν νεκρῶν αὐτοὺς ἔπεισεν, ὅτι ἔσται
   ἐλπὶς τῷ Ἰσραὴλ καὶ ὧδε καὶ ἐπὶ τοῦ μέλλοντος.
14 Οὗτος ἐκεῖ ὢν ἐδείκνυ τῷ λαῷ Ἰσραὴλ τὰ ἐν Ἱερουσαλὴμ καὶ
15 ἐν τῷ ναῷ γινόμενα. οὗτος ἡρπάγη ἐκεῖθεν καὶ ἦλθεν εἰς
   Ἱερουσαλὴμ εἰς ἔλεγχον τῶν ἀπίστων.
16 Οὗτος κατὰ τὸν Μωϋσὴν εἶδεν τὸν τύπον *τοῦ ναοῦ,[22] καὶ[23]
   τὸ τεῖχος καὶ περίτειχος πλατύ, καθὼς εἶπεν καὶ ὁ Δανιήλ, ὅτι
   κτισθήσεται.

---

[18] Corrupted from Ναούρ, Nahor. Both O. T. and N. T. give always the
transliteration Ναχώρ.
[19] The ὅτι mistranslates Heb. *ăsher*, the relative pronoun. Syr. renders
*so that*.
[20] MS adds καί, D and E put the καί after ἐπιπέδου.
[21] The ὥστε renders Heb. *ăsher l'*.
[22] MS om.
[23] MS οὗ, so also E1.

[ 23 ]

17   Οὗτος ἔκρινεν ἐν Βαβυλῶνι τὴν φυλὴν Δὰν καὶ τοῦ Γάδ, ὅτι
     ἠσέβουν εἰς τὸν κύριον διώκοντες τοὺς τὸν νόμον φυλάσσοντας,
18   καὶ ἐποίησεν αὐτοῖς τέρας μέγα, ὅτι οἱ ὄφεις ἀνήλισκον τὰ
19   βρέφη αὐτῶν καὶ πάντα τὰ κτήνη αὐτῶν, καὶ προείρηκεν, ὅτι δι᾽
     αὐτοὺς οὐκ ἐπιστρέψει ὁ λαὸς εἰς τὴν γῆν αὐτοῦ, ἀλλ᾽ ἐν Μηδίᾳ
20   ἔσονται ἕως συντελείας πλάνης αὐτῶν. καὶ ἐξ αὐτῶν ἦν ὁ
     ἀνελὼν αὐτόν· ἀντέκειντο γὰρ αὐτῷ πάσας τὰς ἡμέρας τῆς
     ζωῆς αὐτοῦ.


                              Δ α ν ι ή λ

1    Οὗτος μὲν ἦν ἐκ φυλῆς Ἰουδά, γένους τῶν ἐξεχόντων τῆς
     βασιλικῆς ὑπηρεσίας, ἀλλ᾽ ἔτι νήπιος ἤχθη ἐκ τῆς Ἰουδαίας εἰς
2    γῆν Χαλδαίων²⁴· ἐγεννήθη δὲ ἐν Βεθωρὼν τῇ ἀνωτέρᾳ· καὶ ἦν
     ἀνὴρ σώφρων, ὥστε δοκεῖν τοὺς Ἰουδαίους εἶναι αὐτὸν σπάδοντα.
3    Πολλὰ ἐπένθησεν οὗτος ἐπὶ τὴν πόλιν, καὶ ἐν νηστείαις
     ἤσκησεν ἀπὸ πάσης τροφῆς ἐπιθυμητῆς, καὶ ἦν ἀνὴρ ξηρὸς
     τὴν ἰδέαν, ἀλλὰ ὡραῖος ἐν χάριτι ὑψίστου.
4    Οὗτος πολλὰ ηὔξατο ὑπὲρ τοῦ Ναβουχοδονόσορ, παρακα-
     λοῦντος αὐτὸν Βαλτάσαρ τοῦ υἱοῦ αὐτοῦ, ὅτε ἐγένετο θηρίον καὶ
5    κτῆνος, ἵνα μὴ ἀπόληται. ἦν τὰ ἐμπρόσθια ὡς βοῦς σὺν τῇ
6    κεφαλῇ, καὶ οἱ πόδες σὺν τοῖς ὀπισθίοις ὡς²⁵ λέων. ἀπεκαλύφθη
     τῷ ὁσίῳ περὶ τοῦ μυστηρίου τούτου, ὅτι κτῆνος γέγονε διὰ τὴν
7    φιληδονίαν καὶ τὸ σκληροτράχηλον. καὶ ταῦτα ἔχουσιν οἱ
     δυνάσται ἐν νεότητι, *ὅτι ὡς βοῦς ὑπὸ ζυγὸν γίνονται τοῦ
     Βελίαρ,²⁶ ἐπὶ τέλει δὲ θῆρες γίνονται, ἁρπάζοντες, ὀλεθρεύ-
     οντες, ἀναιροῦντες καὶ πατάσσοντες.
8    Ἔγνω διὰ θεοῦ ὁ ἅγιος, ὅτι ὡς βοῦς ἤσθιε χόρτον καὶ
9    ἐγίνετο αὐτῷ²⁷ ἀνθρωπίνης φύσεως τροφή. διὰ τοῦτο καὶ ὁ
     Ναβουχοδονόσορ μετὰ τὴν πέψιν ἐν καρδίᾳ ἀνθρωπίνῃ γενόμενος
     ἔκλαιεν καὶ ἠξίου κύριον πᾶσαν ἡμέραν καὶ νύκτα τεσσαρακον-
10   τάκις δεόμενος.²⁸ καρδία κτηνῶν ἐπεγίνετο αὐτῷ καὶ ἐλάνθανεν

²⁴ See note 17.
²⁵ MS and D om.
²⁶ MS and D insert this clause between καὶ and ταῦτα.
²⁷ MS om.
²⁸ Period after δεόμενος, as MS, D, and Syr. recognize (passage wanting
in E1), the next sentence beginning with an impossible Βεημωθ or Βεημων.
D emends to Δαίμων δὲ, or (Neap. Syn.) Καὶ ἐλεήμων. Syr., *And he was in*

11 αὐτὸν[29] ὅτι γέγονεν ἄνθρωπος· ἤρθη ἡ γλῶσσα αὐτοῦ τοῦ μὴ
λαλεῖν· καὶ νοῶν εὐθέως ἐδάκρυε,[30] καὶ οἱ ὀφθαλμοὶ αὐτοῦ ἦσαν
12 ὡς κρέας ἐκ τοῦ κλαίειν. πολλοὶ γὰρ ἐξιόντες ἐκ τῆς πόλεως
ἑώρων αὐτόν· ὁ Δανιὴλ μόνος οὐκ ἠθέλησεν αὐτὸν ἰδεῖν, ὅτι
πάντα τὸν χρόνον τῆς ἀλλοιώσεως αὐτοῦ ἐν προσευχῇ ἦν περὶ
13 αὐτοῦ· ἔλεγεν ὅτι πάλιν ἄνθρωπος γενήσεται· καὶ ἠπίστουν
αὐτῷ.
14 Ὁ Δανιὴλ τὰ ἑπτὰ ἔτη, ἃ εἶπεν ἑπτὰ καιρούς, ἐποίησεν
15 γενέσθαι ἑπτὰ μῆνας. τὸ μυστήριον τῶν ἑπτὰ καιρῶν ἐτελέσθη
ἐπ' αὐτόν, ὅτι ἀπεκατέστησεν ἐν[31] ἑπτὰ μησί, τὰ ἓξ ἔτη καὶ
ἓξ[32] μῆνας ὑπέπιπτε κυρίῳ καὶ ὡμολόγει τὴν ἀσέβειαν αὐτοῦ·
καὶ μετὰ ἄφεσιν τῆς ἀνομίας αὐτοῦ ἀπέδωκεν αὐτῷ τὴν βασι-
16 λείαν. οὔτε ἄρτον ἢ κρέα ἔφαγεν οὔτε οἶνον ἔπιεν ἐξομολογού-
μενος, ὅτι ὁ Δανιὴλ αὐτῷ προσέταξεν ἐν ὀσπρίοις βρεκτοῖς καὶ
17 χλόαις ἐξιλεοῦσθαι κύριον. διὰ τοῦτο ἐκάλεσεν αὐτὸν Βαλ-
τάσαρ, ὅτι ἠθέλησεν αὐτὸν συγκληρόνομον καταστῆσαι τῶν
18 τέκνων αὐτοῦ. ἀλλ' ὁ ὅσιος εἶπεν, ἵλεώς μοι ἀφεῖναι κληρο-
νομίαν πατέρων μου καὶ κολληθῆναι κληρονομίαις ἀπεριτμήτων.
19 καὶ τοῖς ἄλλοις βασιλεῦσι Περσῶν πολλὰ ἐποίησεν τεράστια,
20 ὅσα οὐκ ἔγραψαν. ἐκεῖ ἀπέθανε καὶ ἐτάφη ἐν τῷ σπηλαίῳ τῷ
βασιλικῷ μόνος ἐνδόξως.
21 Καὶ αὐτὸς ἔδωκε τέρας ἐν ὄρεσι τοῖς ὑπεράνω Βαβυλῶνος,
ὅτι, ὅτε καπνισθήσεται τὸ ἐκ βορρᾶ, ἥξει τὸ τέλος Βαβυλῶνος·
ὅτε δὲ ὡς ἐν πυρὶ καίεται,[33] τὸ τέλος πάσης τῆς γῆς· ἐὰν δὲ τὸ
ἐν τῷ νότῳ ῥεύσῃ ὕδατα, ἐπιστρέψει ὁ λαὸς εἰς γῆν αὐτοῦ, καὶ
22 ἐὰν αἷμα ῥεύσει, φόνος ἔσται τοῦ Βελίαρ ἐν πάσῃ τῇ γῇ. καὶ
ἐκοιμήθη ἐν εἰρήνῃ ὁ ὅσιος.

the likeness of Behemoth. The reading of E has been a famous puzzle, τεσσα-
ρακοντάκις δεόμενος τοῦ θεοῦ Βεημών, ὅ ἐστι τοῦ θεοῦ Ἰσραήλ. ἐπεγίνετο
γὰρ αὐτῷ πνεῦμα Σατὰν καὶ ἐλάνθανεν αὐτὸν, κτλ.
The narrative has just said that the king had his lucid intervals, ἐν καρδίᾳ
ἀνθρωπίνῃ. Generally, however, the mind of dumb beasts (καρδία κτηνῶν,
Heb. lēb behĕmōth), would have possession of him. Evidently the word for
"heart" had fallen out of the Heb. text. If the original of δεόμενος was
mithpallēl, the accidental omission of lb between l and b would be an error of
a very common sort.

[29] MS and D om.　　　　[30] MS ἐδάκρυσεν.
[31] MS om.; D ἐν ἑπτὰ μησίν, E ἑπτὰ μεσίτας (or μεσίτης).
[32] D πέντε (probably the true reading).　　　　[33] MS κεῖται.

# Ω σ η έ

1 Οὗτος ἦν ἐκ Βελεμὼθ[34] τῆς φυλῆς Ἰσσάχαρ, καὶ ἐτάφη ἐν
2 τῇ γῇ αὐτοῦ ἐν εἰρήνῃ. καὶ ἔδωκε τέρας, ἥξειν κύριος ἐπὶ τῆς
γῆς, ἐὰν ἡ δρῦς ἡ ἐν Σηλὼμ[35] μερισθῇ ἀφ᾽ ἑαυτῆς καὶ γένωνται
δρύες δώδεκα.

# Μ ι χ α ί α ς  ὁ  Μ ω ρ α θ ί[36]

1 ἦν ἐκ φυλῆς Ἐφραίμ. πολλὰ ποιήσας τῷ Ἀχαὰβ ὑπὸ
Ἰωρὰμ τοῦ υἱοῦ αὐτοῦ ἀνῃρέθη κρημνωθείς,[37] ὅτι ἤλεγχεν αὐτὸν
2 ἐπὶ ταῖς ἀσεβείαις τῶν πατέρων αὐτοῦ. καὶ ἐτάφη ἐν τῇ γῇ
αὐτοῦ μόνος σύνεγγυς πολυανδρίου Ἐνακείμ.[38]

# Ἀ μ ὼ ς

1 ἦν ἐκ Θεκουέ. καὶ Ἀμασίας πυκνῶς αὐτὸν τυμπανίσας, τέλος
καὶ ἀνεῖλεν αὐτὸν ὁ υἱὸς αὐτοῦ ἐν ῥοπάλῳ πλήξας αὐτοῦ τὸν
2 κρόταφον· καὶ ἔτι ἐμπνέων ἦλθεν εἰς τὴν γῆν αὐτοῦ καὶ μεθ᾽
ἡμέρας ἀπέθανε καὶ ἐτάφη ἐκεῖ.

# Ἰ ω ὴ λ

1 ἦν ἐκ τῆς γῆς τοῦ Ῥουβὴν ἐν ἀγρῷ Βεθμαών.[39] ἐν εἰρήνῃ
ἀπέθανε καὶ ἐτάφη ἐκεῖ.

# Ἀ β δ ι ο ῦ

1, 2 ἦν ἐκ γῆς Συχὲμ ἀγροῦ Βηθαχαράμ.[40] οὗτος ἦν μαθητὴς
3 Ἡλία καὶ πολλὰ ὑπομείνας δι᾽ αὐτὸν περιεσώζετο. οὗτος ἦν

[34] Cf. Judith 4 4; 7 3; 8 3, Βελμάιμ, Βαλαμών, etc., and see the Translation.
[35] Thus written also in the Life of Ahijah, below, and occasionally in the LXX.
[36] Properly Μωρασθί, see however LXX of Mic 1 1 and Jer 26 18 (33 18).
[37] MS κρημνῷ.
[38] In place of Ἐνακείμ, Syr. has "in Bōkīm."
[39] MS Βεθωμορων, apparently a mixture obtained from Βεθμαών and Βεθωρών. In E, Βηθωμ in one line is followed by ορων one or two lines below. See the Translation.
[40] E Βηθθαχάμαρ, Syr. Beth'agram. Observe that for ἐκ γῆς MS has ἐγγύς.

ὁ τρίτος πεντηκόνταρχος, οὗ ἐφείσατο Ἠλίας καὶ κατέβη πρὸς
4 Ὀχοζίαν. μετὰ ταῦτα ἀπολιπὼν τὴν λειτουργίαν τοῦ βασιλέως
προεφήτευσε καὶ ἀπέθανε ταφεὶς μετὰ τῶν πατέρων αὐτοῦ.

## Ἰωνᾶς

1 ἦν ἐκ γῆς Καριαθμαοῦς⁴¹ πλησίον πόλεως Ἑλλήνων Ἀζώτου⁴²
2 κατὰ θάλασσαν. καὶ ἐκβρασθεὶς ἐκ τοῦ κήτους καὶ ἀπελθὼν ἐν
Νινευῇ ἀνακάμψας οὐκ ἔμεινεν εἰς τὴν γῆν αὐτοῦ, ἀλλὰ παρα-
λαβὼν τὴν μητέρα αὐτοῦ παρῴκησε τὴν Σοὺρ χώραν ἀλλο-
3 φύλων⁴³· ἔλεγε γὰρ, ὅτι οὕτως ἀφελῶ ὄνειδός μου, ὅτι ἐψευσάμην
προφητεύσας κατὰ Νινευῆ τῆς μεγάλης πόλεως.
4 Ἦν τότε Ἠλίας ἐλέγχων τὸν οἶκον Ἀχαάβ, καὶ καλέσας
λιμὸν ἐπὶ τὴν γῆν ἔφυγεν καὶ ἐλθὼν εὗρε τὴν χήραν μετὰ τοῦ
5 υἱοῦ αὐτῆς, οὐ γὰρ ἐδύνατο μένειν μετὰ ἀπεριτμήτων. καὶ
εὐλόγησεν αὐτήν· καὶ θανόντα τὸν υἱὸν αὐτῆς πάλιν ἤγειρεν
ἐκ νεκρῶν ὁ θεὸς διὰ τοῦ Ἠλία, ἠθέλησε γὰρ δεῖξαι αὐτῷ,
ὅτι οὐ δύναται ἀποδρᾶσαι θεόν.⁴⁴
6 Καὶ ἀναστὰς μετὰ τὸν λιμὸν ἦλθεν ἐν γῇ Ἰούδα. καὶ ἀπο-
θανοῦσαν τὴν μητέρα αὐτοῦ κατὰ τὴν ὁδὸν ἔθαψεν αὐτὴν
7 ἐχόμενα τῆς βαλάνου Δεββώρας. καὶ κατοικήσας ἐν γῇ Σα-
ραάρ⁴⁵ ἀπέθανε καὶ ἐτάφη ἐν σπηλαίῳ τοῦ⁴⁶ Κενεζαίου κριτοῦ
8 γενομένου μιᾶς φυλῆς⁴⁷ ἐν ἡμέραις τῆς ἀναρχίας. καὶ ἔδωκε

---

⁴¹ Thus MS and D. E Καριαθμαούμ, Syr. Quryathīm. Some texts have
Καριαθιαρίμ(!).
⁴² Syr. Ekron.
⁴³ MS and D add the interpretation ἐθνῶν. Syr. he dwelt in Sharūb [Sa-
repta?], region of Tyre and Sidon.
⁴⁴ Thus MS. The other texts have been altered more or less by contamination
from the rabbinical legend which identifies Jonah with the child raised to life
in I Ki 17 17 ff. See the note on the Translation. D and E1 merely insert
Ἰωνᾶν before πάλιν ἐκ νεκρῶν. Syr. likewise, and he blessed her and her son
Jonah, and after he died God raised him from the dead. E revises the whole
story, making it begin with the events of I Ki 17 and the childhood of Jonah,
and then bringing the prophet back to Phoenicia after his false prophecy at
Nineveh.
⁴⁵ MS Σαραάρ; D, E, E1, Σαάρ; Syr. Se'īr.
⁴⁶ Article omitted in MS and D (passage abridged and defective in E1).
⁴⁷ "Judge of one tribe" is the original Greek translation, but the Heb. text
was corrupt; instead of shōfēṭ eḥād, "the first judge," it had been made to

τέρας ἐπὶ Ἰερουσαλὴμ καὶ ὅλην τὴν γῆν, ὅτε ἴδωσι λίθον βοῶντα οἰκτρῶς, ἐγγίζειν τὸ τέλος· καὶ ὅτε ἴδωσιν ἐν Ἰερουσαλὴμ πάντα τὰ ἔθνη, ὅτι ἡ πόλις ἕως ἐδάφους ἀφανισθήσεται.[48]

## Ν α ο ὺ μ

1  ἦν[49] ἀπὸ Ἐλκεσὶ[50] πέραν τοῦ [ὄρους] εἰς Βηθγαβρὶν[51] φυλῆς
2  Συμεών. οὗτος μετὰ τὸν Ἰωνᾶν τῇ Νινευῇ τέρας ἔδωκεν, ὅτι ὑπὸ ὑδάτων γλυκίων καὶ πυρὸς ὑπογείου[52] ἀπολεῖται, ὃ καὶ
3  γέγονεν. ἡ γὰρ περιέχουσα αὐτὴν λίμνη κατέκλυσεν αὐτὴν ἐν σεισμῷ, καὶ πῦρ ἐκ τῆς ἐρήμου ἐπελθὸν τὸ ὑψηλότερον αὐτῆς
4  μέρος ἐνέπρησεν. ἀπέθανε δὲ ἐν εἰρήνῃ καὶ ἐτάφη ἐν τῇ γῇ αὐτοῦ.

## Ἀ μ β α κ ο ὺ μ

1, 2  ἐκ φυλῆς ἦν Συμεὼν ἐξ ἀγροῦ Βηθζουχάρ.[53] οὗτος εἶδε πρὸ τῆς αἰχμαλωσίας περὶ τῆς ἁλώσεως Ἰερουσαλὴμ καὶ ἐπένθησε
3  σφόδρα. καὶ ὅτε ἦλθε Ναβουχοδονόσορ ἐν Ἰερουσαλήμ, ἔφυγεν
4  εἰς Ὀστρακίνην καὶ παρῴκησεν ἐν γῇ Ἰσμαήλ. ὡς δὲ ἐπέστρεψαν[54] οἱ Χαλδαῖοι, καὶ οἱ κατάλοιποι οἱ ὄντες ἐν Ἰερουσαλὴμ κατέβησαν[55] εἰς Αἴγυπτον, ἦν παροικῶν τὴν γῆν αὐτοῦ.

5, 6  Καὶ ἐλειτούργει θερισταῖς τοῦ ἀγροῦ αὐτοῦ· ὡς δὲ ἔλαβε τὸ ἔδεσμα, προεφήτευσε τοῖς ἰδίοις εἰπών· πορεύομαι εἰς γῆν μακρὰν καὶ ταχέως ἐλεύσομαι· εἰ δὲ βραδύνω, ἀπενέγκατε τοῖς
7  θερισταῖς. καὶ γενόμενος ἐν Βαβυλῶνι καὶ δοὺς τὸ ἄριστον τῷ Δανιὴλ ἐπέστη τοῖς θερισταῖς ἐσθίουσι καὶ οὐδενὶ εἶπεν τὸ γενόμενον.

read *shōfēṭ shevēṭ eḥād*, "the judge of one tribe." MS, D, and Syr. have the false reading, the other texts omit the words. The two Hebrew nouns are several times confused in the O. T.

[48] MS ἡφάνισται ὅλη.
[49] MS om.
[50] See the LXX.
[51] MS πέραν τοῦ Ἰσβηγαβαρίν, Ε πέραν τοῦ Ἰορδάνου εἰς Βηγαβάρ, Ε1 ἀπὸ Ἰεσβή, D πέραν τοῦ εἰς Βηταβαρήν, Syr. *on the other side of Beth-ḥawarīm*.
[52] MS ὑπογίου, Ε ἐπιγείου.
[53] D Βηθιτουχάρ, Ε Βυζζουχάρ, Ε1 Βιδζουχάρ, Syr. *Beth-sūkar*.
[54] D, Ε, ὑπέστρεψαν.
[55] MS om.

Συνῆκεν δὲ ὅτι τάχειον ἐπιστρέψει ὁ λαὸς ἀπὸ Βαβυλῶνος.
9 καὶ πρὸ δύο ἐτῶν ἀποθνήσκει τῆς ἐπιστροφῆς. καὶ ἐτάφη ἐν
ἀγρῷ ἰδίῳ μόνος.
10 Ἔδωκε δὲ τέρας τοῖς ἐν τῇ Ἰουδαίᾳ, ὅτι ὄψονται ἐν τῷ ναῷ
11 φῶς, καὶ οὕτως ἴδωσι τὴν δόξαν τοῦ ναοῦ.⁵⁶ καὶ περὶ συντελείας
12 τοῦ ναοῦ προεῖπεν, ὅτι ὑπὸ ἔθνους δυτικοῦ γενήσεται. τότε τὸ⁵⁷
ἅπλωμα, φησί, τοῦ δαβεὶρ εἰς μικρὰ ῥαγήσεται, καὶ τὰ ἐπίκρανα
τῶν δύο στύλων ἀφαιρεθήσονται καὶ οὐδεὶς γνώσεται, ποῦ
13 ἔσονται· αὐτὰ δὲ ἐν τῇ ἐρήμῳ ἀπενεχθήσονται ὑπὸ ἀγγέλων,
14 ὅπου ἐν ἀρχῇ ἐπάγη ἡ σκηνὴ τοῦ μαρτυρίου. καὶ ἐν αὐτοῖς
γνωσθήσεται ἐπὶ τέλει κύριος, ὅτι φωτίσουσι τοὺς διωκομένους
ὑπὸ τοῦ ὄφεως ἐν σκότει ὡς ἐξ ἀρχῆς.

## Σοφονίας

1, 2 ἐκ φυλῆς ἦν Συμεὼν ἀγροῦ Σαβαραθά·⁵⁸ προεφήτευσε περὶ
3 τῆς πόλεως καὶ περὶ τέλους ἐθνῶν καὶ αἰσχύνης ἀσεβῶν· καὶ
θανὼν ἐτάφη ἐν ἀγρῷ αὐτοῦ.

## Ἀγγαῖος

1 τάχα νέος ἦλθεν ἐκ Βαβυλῶνος εἰς Ἱερουσαλὴμ καὶ φανερῶς
περὶ τῆς ἐπιστροφῆς τοῦ λαοῦ προεφήτευσε καὶ εἶδεν ἐκ μέρους
2 τὴν οἰκοδομὴν τοῦ ναοῦ· καὶ θανὼν ἐτάφη πλησίον τοῦ τάφου
τῶν ἱερέων ἐνδόξως ὡς αὐτοί.

## Ζαχαρίας

1 ἦλθεν ἀπὸ Χαλδαίων ἤδη προβεβηκὼς καὶ ἐκεῖ πολλὰ τῷ λαῷ
2 προεφήτευσε· καὶ τέρατα ἔδωκεν εἰς ἀπόδειξιν. οὗτος εἶπε τῷ
Ἰωσεδέκ, ὅτι γεννήσει υἱὸν καὶ ἐν Ἱερουσαλὴμ ἱερατεύσει·
3 οὗτος καὶ τὸν Σαλαθιὴλ ἐφ' υἱῷ εὐλόγησε καὶ ὄνομα Ζοροβάβελ
4 ἐπέθηκε. καὶ ἐπὶ Κύρου τέρας ἔδωκεν εἰς νῖκος καὶ περὶ τῆς
λειτουργίας αὐτοῦ προηγόρευσεν, ἣν ποιήσει ἐπὶ Ἱερουσαλήμ,

---

⁵⁶ E θεοῦ, passage omitted in D.
⁵⁷ MS om.
⁵⁸ D Σαβαρθαθά, E Σαραβαθά.

5  καὶ ηὐλόγησεν αὐτὸν σφόδρα. τὰ δὲ τῆς προφητείας ἐν
   Ἰερουσαλήμ[59] καὶ περὶ τέλους ἐθνῶν καὶ Ἰσραὴλ καὶ τοῦ ναοῦ καὶ
   ἀργίας προφητῶν καὶ ἱερέων καὶ περὶ διπλῆς κρίσεως ἐξέθετο.
6  καὶ ἀπέθανεν[60] ἐν γήρει μακρῷ καὶ ἐκλιπὼν ἐτάφη σύνεγγυς
   Ἀγγαίου.

### · Μ α λ α χ ί α ς

1  Οὗτος μετὰ τὴν ἐπιστροφὴν τίκτεται ἐν Σωφᾶ,[61] καὶ ἔτι πάνυ
2  νέος καλὸν βίον ἔσχηκε. καὶ ἐπειδὴ πᾶς ὁ λαὸς ἐτίμα αὐτὸν ὡς
   ὅσιον καὶ πρᾳῦν, ἐκάλεσαν αὐτὸν Μαλαχί, ὃ ἑρμηνεύεται
3  ἄγγελος·[62] ἦν γὰρ καὶ τῷ ἰδεῖν εὐπρεπής. ἀλλὰ καὶ ὅσα εἶπεν
   αὐτὸς ἐν προφητείᾳ, αὐτῇ τῇ ἡμέρᾳ ὀφθεὶς ἄγγελος θεοῦ ἐπεδευ-
   τέρωσεν, ὡς ἐγένετο ἐν ἡμέραις ἀναρχίας, ὡς γέγραπται ἐν
4  Σφαρφωτίμ,[63] τουτέστιν ἐν βίβλῳ Κριτῶν.[62] καὶ ἔτι νέος
   προσετέθη πρὸς τοὺς πατέρας αὐτοῦ ἐν ἀγρῷ αὐτοῦ.

### Ν α θ ὰ ν

1  προφήτης Δαυὶδ ἦν ἐκ Γαβαών,[64] ἐκ φυλῆς Ἐωή.[65] καὶ αὐτὸς
2  ἦν ὁ διδάξας αὐτὸν νόμον κυρίου. καὶ εἶδεν ὅτι Δαυὶδ ἐν τῇ
   Βηρσαβεὲ[66] παραβήσεται, καὶ σπεύδοντα ἐλθεῖν ἀγγεῖλαι αὐτῷ
   ἐνεπόδισεν ὁ Βελίαρ, ὅτι κατὰ τὴν ὁδὸν εὗρεν νεκρὸν καίμενον
3  γυμνὸν ἐσφαγμένον· καὶ ἐπέμεινεν ἐκεῖ καὶ τῇ νυκτὶ ἐκείνῃ ἔγνω,
4  ὅτι ἐποίησε τὴν ἁμαρτίαν· καὶ ὑπέστρεψε πενθῶν. καὶ ὡς ἀνεῖλε
5  τὸν ἄνδρα αὐτῆς, ἔπεμψε κύριος ἐλέγξαι αὐτόν. καὶ αὐτὸς πάνυ
   γηράσας ἀπέθανεν καὶ ἐτάφη εἰς τὴν γῆν αὐτοῦ.

[59] MS καὶ εὐλόγησεν αὐτόν. σφόδρα δὲ τῆς προφητείας ἴδεν ἐν Ἰερουσαλήμ, κτλ. D also has the verb εἶδεν.

[60] Syr. wethkerah, presumably rendering καὶ ἠσθένησεν, which is the reading evidently required by our Grk. text. The other recensions omit ἐκλιπών.

[61] D, E, E1, Σοφᾶ, Syr. Sōphā.

[62] Clause added by the Grk. translator; cf. John 1 38, 41, etc.

[63] Scribal corruption of Σφαρσωφτίμ. E Σφαρφωθίμ, Syr. sfarfoṭmīn, D
Σφαρτελλείμ (the Psalter), E1 wanting.

[64] As in D and Syr. MS Γαβᾶ, E Γαβάθ, E1 wanting.

[65] Clause preserved only in E, where however the name of the "tribe"
(Ἐωη, transliterating Heb. Ḥwi) is miswritten as Θωη.

[66] Thus ("Beersheba") in all the Grk. texts, Syr. alone giving the true name.

# Ἀχία

1 ἀπὸ Σηλώμ,[67] ὅπου ἦν ἡ σκηνὴ τὸ παλαιόν, ἐκ πόλεως Ἠλί.
2, 3 οὗτος εἶπε περὶ Σαλωμών, ὅτι προσκρούσει κυρίῳ· καὶ ἤλεγξε
τὸν Ἱεροβοάμ, ὅτι δόλῳ ἐπορεύετο[68] μετὰ κυρίου· εἶδεν ζεῦγος
4 βοῶν πατοῦντα τὸν λαὸν καὶ κατὰ τῶν ἱερέων ἐπιτρέχοντα· προ-
εἶπε καὶ τῷ Σαλωμών, ὅτι αἱ γυναῖκες αὐτὸν ἐκστήσουσι καὶ
5 πᾶν τὸ γένος αὐτοῦ. καὶ ἀπέθανε καὶ ἐτάφη σύνεγγυς τῆς δρυὸς
Σηλώμ.

# Ἰωὴδ[69]

1 ἦν[70] ἐκ γῆς[71] Σαμαρείμ.[72] οὗτος ἐστίν, ὃν ἐπάταξεν ὁ λέων καὶ
2 ἀπέθανεν, ὅτε ἤλεγξεν τὸν Ἱεροβοὰμ ἐπὶ ταῖς δαμάλεσι· καὶ
ἐτάφη ἐν Βεθὴλ σύνεγγυς[73] τοῦ ψευδοπροφήτου τοῦ πλανήσαντος
αὐτόν.

# Ἀζαρίας

1 ἦν ἐκ γῆς Συβαθά,[74] ὃς ἐπέστρεψεν ἐξ Ἰσραὴλ τὴν αἰχμα-
2 λωσίαν Ἰούδα.[75] καὶ θανὼν ἐτάφη ἐν ἀγρῷ αὐτοῦ.

# Ζαχαρίας[76]

1 ἐξ Ἱερουσαλήμ, υἱὸς Ἰωδαὲ τοῦ ἱερέως, ὃν ἀπέκτεινεν Ἰωὰς ὁ
Βασιλεὺς Ἰούδα ἐχόμενα τοῦ θυσιαστηρίου, καὶ ἐξέχεεν τὸ αἷμα
αὐτοῦ ὁ οἶκος Δαυὶδ ἀνὰ μέσον ἐπὶ τοῦ αἰλάμ· καὶ λαβόντες
2 αὐτὸν οἱ ἱερεῖς ἔθαψαν αὐτὸν μετὰ τοῦ πατρὸς αὐτοῦ· ἔκτοτε

---

67 See note 35.
68 MS πορεύσεται.
69 MS Ἰωάδ, D Ἰωάθ, E and Syr. Ἰωάμ.
70 MS om.
71 MS τῆς.
72 D Σαμαρίν, E ἐγεννήθη ἐν Σαμαρείᾳ.
73 Syr. by the side of Abīi̭ōn, the false prophet, etc.
74 D Συνβαθά, E Συμβαθά, Syr. Seqūtha (for Sebūtha?).
75 "Israel" and "Judah" transposed, the mistake made in the Hebrew original; see the Translation.
76 E1, which after the Twelve Minor Prophets has only Elijah and Elisha,
introduces the life of this Zechariah as the second half of the biography of
Zechariah ben Iddo.

ἐγένοντο τέρατα ἐν τῷ ναῷ φαντασίας καὶ οὐκ ἴσχυον οἱ
ἱερεῖς ἰδεῖν ὀπτασίαν ἀγγέλων θεοῦ οὔτε δοῦναι χρησμοὺς ἐκ
τοῦ δαβεὶρ οὔτε ἐρωτῆσαι ἐν τῷ ἐφοὺδ οὔτε διὰ δήλων
ἀποκριθῆναι τῷ λαῷ ὡς τὸ πρίν.

## Ἡλίας

1 Θεσβίτης ἦν[77] ἐκ γῆς Ἀράβων,[78] φυλῆς Ἀαρών, οἰκῶν ἐν
2 Γαλαάδ, ὅτι ἡ Θεσβεὶ[79] δόμα ἦν τοῖς ἱεροῦσιν. ὅτε εἶχεν τεχ-
θῆναι, εἶδεν Σοβαχὰ[80] ὁ πατὴρ αὐτοῦ, ὅτι ἄνδρες λευκοφανεῖς
αὐτὸν προσηγόρευον, καὶ ὅτι ἐν πυρὶ αὐτὸν ἐσπαργάνουν καὶ
3 φλόγα πυρὸς ἐδίδουν αὐτῷ φαγεῖν· καὶ ἐλθὼν ἀνήγγειλεν ἐν
Ἰερουσαλήμ, καὶ εἶπεν αὐτῷ ὁ χρησμός· μὴ δειλιάσῃς· ἔσται
γὰρ ἡ οἴκησις αὐτοῦ φῶς καὶ ὁ λόγος αὐτοῦ ἀπόφασις, καὶ
κρινεῖ τὸν Ἰσραὴλ* ἐν ῥομφαίᾳ καὶ ἐν πυρί.[81]

## Ἐλισαῖος

1, 2 Ἐλισαῖος ἦν ἐξ Ἀβελμαοὺλ[82] γῆς τοῦ Ῥουβήν· καὶ ἐπὶ τού-
του γέγονε τέρας, ὅτι, ἡνίκα ἐτέχθη ἐν Γαλγάλοις ἡ δάμαλις ἡ
3 χρυσῆ ὀξὺν ἐβόησεν, ὥστε ἀκουσθῆναι εἰς Ἰερουσαλήμ· καὶ εἶπεν
ὁ ἱερεὺς διὰ τῶν δήλων, ὅτι προφήτης ἐτέχθη Ἰσραήλ, ὃς καθ-
4 ελεῖ τὰ γλυπτὰ αὐτῶν καὶ τὰ χωνευτά. καὶ θανὼν ἐτάφη ἐν
Σαμαρείᾳ.

[77] MS om.
[78] See the note on the Translation. The collocation of Ἀραβῶν with Ἀαρών,
which looks suspicious, is purely accidental.
[79] D, E, E1, Θέσβις. MS and Syr. have the original transliteration (see the
Heb. consonant text in I Ki 17 1).
[80] E Σωβάκ, Syr. Sobach. E1 makes this the name of his mother.
[81] MS om.
[82] The reading of Cod. A in I Ki 4 12 and 19 16. E Ἀβελμούθ (orig. — μα-
ουθ?), E1 Ἀβελμουήλ, D Ἀβελμούλ (Neap. Syn. Ἀβελβουήλ), Syr. Abel-
mechola.

# TRANSLATION

The Names of the Prophets, and
whence they were, where they died,
and how and where they were buried

# ISAIAH

1    He was of Jerusalem. He met his death at the hands of Manasseh, sawn in two,[1] and was buried below the fountain of Rogel,[2] hard by the conduit of the waters which Hezekiah spoiled (for the enemy) by blocking their course.[3]

3    For the prophet's sake God wrought the miracle of Siloah; for before his death, in fainting condition he prayed for water, and it was sent to him from this source. Hence it was called Siloah, which means "sent."[4]

3    Also in the time of Hezekiah, before the king made the pools and the reservoirs,[5] at the prayer of Isaiah a little water came forth here, lest the city, at that time besieged by the Gentiles, 4  should be destroyed through lack of water. For the enemy were seeking a drinking place, and as they invested the city they encamped near Siloah. If then the Hebrews came to the pool, water flowed forth; if the Gentiles came, there was none. Hence even to the present day the water issues suddenly,[6] to keep the miracle in mind.

5    Because this was wrought through the prayer of Isaiah, the people in remembrance buried his body near the spot, with care and high honor, in order that through his prayers, even after his death, they might continue to have the benefit of the water. Indeed, a revelation had been given them concerning 6  him. His tomb, however, is near the tomb of the kings, behind the tomb of the priests on the side toward the south.

[1] Ascension of Isaiah, chap. 5; Heb 11 37; Talm. Yebamoth, 49b.
[2] Josh 18 16, I Ki 1 9.
[3] II Chr 32 3.
[4] Compare John 9 7.
[5] Apparent allusion to the difficult passage Is 22 9–11.
[6] The Virgin's Fountain is an intermittent spring: see, e. g., *Enc. Bibl.* II col. 2414.

7     Solomon constructed the tombs, which had been designed by David, on the east of Zion, where there is an entering road from Gibeon, the town twenty stadia distant from the city. He made a winding construction, its location unsuspected; even to the present day it is unknown to the most of the priests, and wholly unknown to the people.

8     There the king kept the gold and the spices from Ethiopia.

9     When Hezekiah showed to the Gentiles the secret of David and Solomon,[7] and defiled the bones of his ancestors, therefore God laid upon him the curse, that his descendants should be in servitude to their enemies; and God made him to be childless, from that day.

## JEREMIAH

1     He was of Anathoth, and he died in Taphnes[8] in Egypt, stoned

2 to death by the Jews. He is buried in the place where Pharaoh's palace stood;[9] for the Egyptians held him in honor, because of

3 the benefit which they had received through him. For at his prayer, the serpents which the Egyptians call *ephōth*[10] de-

4 parted from them; and even at the present day the faithful servants of God pray on that spot, and taking of the dust of the place they heal the bites of serpents.

5     We have been told by the children of Antigonus and Ptolemy, aged men,[11] that Alexander the Macedonian, when he stood at the place where the prophet was buried, and learned of the wonders which he had wrought, carried away his bones to

6 Alexandria, placing them round about with due ceremony; whereupon the whole race of poisonous serpents was driven out of the land. With like purpose he (the prophet) had introduced into Egypt the so-called *argolai* (that is, "snake-fighters").[10]

7     Jeremiah also gave a sign to the priests of Egypt, that their

[7] II Ki 20 12 ff.

[8] Jer 43 7–13.

[9] Jer 43 9.

[10] See the Appendix, on the Reptiles of the Jeremiah Narrative.

[11] The following tradition was probably narrated by native Egyptians resident in Jerusalem, see the Introduction.

[ 35 ]

idols would be shaken and their gods made with hands would all collapse, when there should arrive in Egypt a virgin bearing
8   a child of divine appearance. Wherefore even to the present time they honor a virgin mother, and placing a babe in a manger they bow down to it. When Ptolemy the king sought the reason for this, they said to him: "It is a mystery handed down from our fathers, a sign delivered to them by a holy prophet, and we are awaiting its fulfiment."[12]

9     This prophet,[13] before the destruction of the temple, took possession of the ark of the law and the things within it, and caused them to be swallowed up in a rocky cliff, and he said to
10  those who were present: "The Lord departed from Sinai into heaven, and he will again come with might; and this shall be for you the sign of his appearance, when all the Gentiles worship a piece of wood."[14]

11     He said also: "No one shall bring forth this ark but Aaron, and the tables within it no one of the priests or prophets shall
12  unfold but Moses the elect of God." And in the resurrection the ark will rise first, and come forth from the rock, and will be placed on Mount Sinai; and all the saints will be assembled to it there, awaiting the Lord and fleeing from the enemy wishing to destroy them.[15]

13     He sealed in the rock with his finger the name of God, and the writing was as though carved with iron. A cloud then covered the name; and no one knows the place, nor can the
14  writing be read, to the present day and even to the end. The rock is in the wilderness where the ark was at first, between the two mountains on which Moses and Aaron are buried, and by night there is a cloud as it were of fire, according to the primal ordinance that the glory of God should never cease from his
15  law. And God gave to Jeremiah the favor of completing this wonder, so that he might be the associate of Moses, and they are together to this day.

---

[12] This Christian passage stood in the original text, see the Introduction.
[13] II Macc 2 4 ff.
[14] The cross.
[15] Compare the last sentences of the Life of the prophet Habakkuk.

# EZEKIEL

1 He was from the district of Sarīra,[16] of the priests; and he died in the land of Chaldea, in the time of the captivity, after
2 uttering many prophecies to those who were in Judea. He was slain by the leader of the Israelite exiles, who had been rebuked by him
3 for his worship of idols; and they buried him in the field of Nahor, in the tomb of Shem and Arphaxad, the ancestors of Abraham.
4 The tomb is a double cave, according to whose plan Abraham
5 also made the tomb of Sarah in Hebron.[17] It is called "double" because it has a winding (stairway) and there is an upper chamber hidden from the main floor,[18] hung in the rock above the ground-level.
6 This prophet gave to the people a sign, that they should pay
7 attention to the river Chebar;[19] when its waters should fail, they were to expect "the sickle of desolation to the ends of the earth";[20] when it should overflow, the return to Jerusalem.
8 While the saint was dwelling there, many kept coming to
9 him; and on one occasion, when a throng had assembled to him, the Chaldeans feared an uprising and came upon them to
10 destroy them. He made the water cease its flow, so that they could flee to the other side; but when the enemy ventured to pursue, they were drowned.
11 Through his prayer he provided for them ample sustenance in fish which came of their own accord to be caught. Many who were at the point of death he cheered with the news of
12 life coming to them from God. When the people were being destroyed by the enemy, he went to the hostile captains and so terrified them with marvels which he wrought that they ceased.
13 It was then that he said to the people:[21] "Are we indeed perishing? is our hope at an end?" and by the vision of the dry bones[22] he persuaded them that there is hope for Israel both now and in the time to come.

[16] The name is known only from this document.
[17] Gen 23 2, 9, 17, 19.
[18] Lit., from the ground.
[19] Ezek 1 1; 3 15; 43 3.     [20] Joel 4 12 f.
[21] Ezek 37 11.     [22] Ezek 37 1 ff.

14     While he was there he showed to the people of Israel what was
15   being done in Jerusalem and in the temple. He himself was
borne away thence, and came to Jerusalem,[23] for a rebuke to the
16   faithless. Also after the manner of Moses[24] he foresaw the fashion
of the temple, with its walls and its broad surroundings, as
Daniel also declared that it should be built.[25]
17     He pronounced judgment in Babylon on the tribes of Dan and
Gad, because they dealt wickedly against the Lord, persecuting
18   those who were keeping the law; and he wrought upon them this
grievous wonder, that their children and all their cattle should
19   be killed by serpents. He also foretold, that because of their
sin Israel would not return to its land but would remain in
Media, until the end of this evildoing.
20     One of their number was the man who slew Ezekiel, for they
opposed him all the days of his life.


## DANIEL

1     He was of the tribe of Judah, of a family prominent in the
service of the king;[26] but in his childhood he was carried away
2   from Judea to the land of Chaldea. He was born in Upper
Beth-horon. In his manhood he was chaste, so that the Jews
thought him a eunuch.
3     He mourned greatly over the city, and in fasting abstained
from every sort of dainty food. He was lean and haggard in the
eyes of men, but beautiful in the grace of the Most High.
4     He made great supplication in behalf of Nebuchadnezzar,
whose son Belshazzar[27] besought him for aid at the time when
the king became a beast of the field, lest he should perish.
5   For his head and foreparts were those of an ox, his legs and
6   hinder parts those of a lion. The meaning of this marvel was
revealed to the prophet: the king became a beast because of his
7   self-indulgence and his stubbornness. It is the manner of tyrants,

[23] Ezek 8 3.
[24] Ex 25 9, 40.
[25] Dan 9 25.
[26] Dan 1 3.
[27] Baltasar in the text.

that in their youth they come under the yoke of Satan;[28] in their latter years they become wild beasts, snatching, destroying, smiting, and slaying.

8 The prophet knew by divine revelation that the king was eating grass like an ox, and that it became for him the food of a human

9 being. Therefore it was that Nebuchadnezzar himself, recovering human reason when digestion was completed, used to weep and beseech the Lord, praying forty times each day and night.

10 Then the mind of a dumb animal[29] would (again) take possession of him and he would forget that he had been a human being.

11 His tongue had lost the power of speech; when he understood his condition he wept, and his eyes were like raw flesh from his weeping.

12 There were many who went out from the city to see him; Daniel alone had no wish to see him, but during all the time of

13 his transformation he was in prayer for him. He declared that the king would be restored to human form, but they did not believe him.

14 Daniel caused the seven years (the meaning of his "seven
15 times")[30] to become seven months. The mystery of the seven times was fulfilled upon the king, for in seven months he was restored, and in the (remaining) six years and five[31] months he was doing penance to the Lord and confessing his wickedness. When his sin had been forgiven, the kingdom was given back to

16 him. He ate neither bread nor flesh in the time of his repentance, for Daniel had bidden him eat pulse and greens while appeasing the Lord.

17 The king named the prophet Baltasar[32] because he wished to
18 make him a joint heir with his children; but the holy man said: "Far be it from me to forsake the heritage of my fathers and join

19 in the inheritances of the uncircumcised." He also did for the other Persian kings many wonderful things which were not

20 written down. He died there, and was buried with great honor, by himself, in the royal sepulcher.

---

[28] The text, Beliar.
[29] Text emended, see the Note.
[30] Dan 4 16, 32 (Heb 4 13, 29).
[31] "Six months" in some texts.  [32] Dan 1 7; 5 12.

[ 39 ]

21    He appointed a sign in the mountains which are above Babylon: When the mountain on the north shall smoke, the end of Babylon will come; when it shall burn as with fire, the end of all the earth will be at hand.  If the mountain on the south shall flow with water, Israel will return to its land; if it shall run blood, it portends a slaughter brought by Satan[33] on all the
22    earth.  And the holy prophet slept in peace.


## HOSEA

1    He was from Belemōth,[34] of the tribe of Issachar, and he was buried in peace, in his own land.
2    He gave a sign, that the Lord would come to the earth when the oak tree which is in Shiloh[35] should of its own accord be divided and become twelve oaks.


## MICAH THE MORASHTITE[36]

1    He was of the tribe of Ephraim.  Having given much trouble to King Ahab, he was killed, thrown from a cliff, by Ahab's son Joram, because he rebuked him for the wickedness of his fathers.
2    He was given solitary burial in his own land, near the burying place of the giants.


## AMOS

1    He was from Tekoa.[37]  Amaziah (the priest of Bethel)[38] had often beaten him, and at last Amaziah's son killed him with a
2    cudgel, striking him on the temple.  While still living he made his way to his land, and after some days died and was buried there.

---

[33] Beliar.
[34] A better reading is Belamon, see the Note on the text.  This is the city which appears also under the names Yible'am, Bile'am, etc.  See Buhl, *Geographie des alten Palästina*, 102, 201 f.
[35] This oak tree appears also in the Life of Ahijah, below.
[36] Micah 1 1.  Buhl, *Geogr.*, 193.
[37] Am 1 1.
[38] Am 7 10 ff.

## JOEL

1   He was from the territory of Reuben, of the field of Beth-meon.[39] He died in peace, and was buried there.

## OBADIAH

1   He was from the region of Shechem, of the field of Beth-
2   hakkerem.[40] He was a pupil of Elijah, and having done much
3   in his service he was saved from death by him. He was that
third captain of fifty whom Elijah spared, and went down with
4   him to Ahaziah. Afterward, leaving the service of the king he
became a prophet,[41] and upon his death he was buried with his
fathers.

## JONAH

1   He was from the district of Kiriath-maon(?),[42] near the
Gentile city of Azotus on the sea.
2   After he had been cast on shore by the whale and had made
his journey to Nineveh, on his return[43] he did not stay in his
own land, but took his mother and settled in Tyre, a country
3   of foreign peoples. For he said, "In this way I will take away
my reproach, that I prophesied falsely against the great city
Nineveh."[44]
4   Elijah was at that time rebuking the house of Ahab, and having
called a famine upon the land he fled.[45] Coming to the region

[39] In the Bible this city is given the names Beth-baal-meon, Beth-meon
(Jer 48 23), Baal-meon, and once simply Be'on; see Buhl, *Geogr.*, 267. It
appears in the Mesha inscription as Ba'al Me'on (9) and Beth-ba'al-me'on
(30). In the mss. of the *Lives* the name is corrupt.
[40] This is not the Beth-haccherem of Jer 6 1 and Neh 3 14, which was in
Judea. "House of the vineyard" might well have been a name frequently
occurring in Palestine.
[41] So in the rabbinical tradition.
[42] Perhaps the most likely form of the name, which is otherwise unknown.
[43] The rabbinical writings have no mention of any return of the prophet
from Nineveh to his own land (Ginzberg, *Legends of the Jews*, VI, 351).
III Macc 6 8 speaks of such a return.
[44] Jon 3 4–10.
[45] I Ki 17 1 f.

[ 41 ]

of Tyre he found the widow and her son, for he himself could
5 not lodge with the uncircumcised. He brought her a blessing;
and when her child died, God raised him from the dead through
Elijah, for he wished to show him⁴⁶ that it is not possible to flee
from God.

6 After the famine was over, Jonah came into the land of
Judea. On the way thither his mother died, and he buried her
7 beside the oak of Deborah.⁴⁷ Thereafter having settled in the
land of Seir,⁴⁸ he died there and was buried in the tomb of the
Kenizzite, the first who became judge⁴⁹ in the days when there
was no king.

8 He gave a sign to Jerusalem and to all the land: When they
should see a stone crying aloud⁵⁰ in distress, the end would be
at hand; and when they should see all the Gentiles gathered in
Jerusalem, the city would be razed to its foundations.

## NAHUM

1 He was of Elkosh,⁵¹ on the other side of the mountains toward
Beth-gabrin,⁵² of the tribe of Simeon.

⁴⁶ That is, Elijah. From this account arose, not unnaturally, the widespread
rabbinical legend that "the son" mentioned in I Ki 17 17 was Jonah (!),
although this is made impossible by the preceding narrative, which evidently
antedates the legend. It is to be observed that in I Kings the LXX has the
plural, "children," in verses 12, 13, and 15, and this is supported by "house-
hold" in the Hebrew of vs. 15. *The plural should probably be read in the Heb.
of vss. 12 and 13.* The popular tradition recorded in the *Lives*, that the widow
of I Ki 17 was Jonah's mother, was therefore not in conflict with the Biblical
narrative. The Greek text of our MS gives the original translation, all the
others are under the influence of the rabbinical story, which is told consistently
in the E version. See the Note on the text.

⁴⁷ Gen 35 8.

⁴⁸ That is, Edom.

⁴⁹ The translation rests on conjectural emendation of the Hebrew text,
see the Note on the Greek. Othniel son of Kenaz was the first of the Judges
of Israel (Jud 3 9–11).

⁵⁰ Hab 2 11.

⁵¹ Nah 1 1.

⁵² The existing texts show plainly that a single word, a masculine noun,
has accidentally fallen out of the Greek translation. Supposing the standpoint of the narrator to be Jerusalem, and the location of Elkosh to be near

2    This prophet after the time of Jonah gave a sign to Nineveh, that it would be destroyed by fresh waters and by underground
3    fire;[53] and indeed this came to pass. For the lake which surrounded the city overwhelmed it in an earthquake, and fire
4    coming from the desert burned its upper portion. He died in peace, and was buried in his land.


## HABAKKUK

1    He was from the tribe of Simeon, of the field of Beth-zachariah.[54]
2    Before the captivity he had a vision of the destruction of
3    Jerusalem, and he grieved exceedingly. When Nebuchadnezzar came against Jerusalem, he fled to Ostracina (in Egypt), and then sojourned in the land of Ishmael.[55]
4    When the Chaldeans returned (to their country), and all those who were left in Jerusalem went down to Egypt,[56] he settled
5    again in his own land. He was accustomed to carry food to the
6    reapers of the harvest in his field;[57] and one day, as he received the food, he announced to his family: "I am off for a far country, but will return immediately; if I should delay, carry out the
7    food to the reapers." Finding himself straightway in Babylon, and having given Daniel his meal, he stood by the reapers as they ate; and he told no one what had happened.
8    He had knowledge that the people would soon come back from
9    Babylon. Two years before the return he died, and was buried alone in his own field.
10   He gave a sign to the people in Judea, that they would see in the temple a light shining, and thus they would know the

Beth-gabrin (Eleutheropolis), it is plain that the latter cities are "on the other side" of one of the mountain ridges of Judea. It is reasonable conjecture that "mountain" was the missing word, and no other solution equally plausible suggests itself.

[53] Nah 2 6–8; 3 15.
[54] I Macc 6 32 ff., Buhl, *Geogr.*, 159.
[55] Arabia.
[56] II Ki 25 26.
[57] The following in Bel and the Dragon, 33 ff.

11 glory of the sanctuary. Concerning the end of the temple, he
foretold that it would be brought to pass by a western nation.
12 Then, he said, the veil of the inner sanctuary will be torn to
pieces, and the capitals of the two pillars will be taken away,
13 and no one will know where they are; but they will be carried
away by angels into the wilderness where in the beginning the
14 Tabernacle of Witness was pitched. By them in the end the
presence of the Lord will be made known, for they will give
light to those who are pursued by the Serpent[58] in darkness as at
the beginning.

## ZEPHANIAH

1 He was of the tribe of Simeon, of the field of Sabaratha (?).[59]
2 He prophesied concerning the city, also concerning the end of
3 the nations and the confounding of the wicked. When he died
he was buried in his own field.

## HAGGAI

1 Probably as a youth he came from Babylon to Jerusalem, and
he had prophesied publicly in regard to the return of the people.
2 He witnessed in part the building of the temple. Upon his death
he was buried near the tomb of the priests, honored as though
one of their number.

## ZECHARIAH SON OF IDDO

1 He came from Chaldea[60] when already advanced in age. While
there, he prophesied often to the people, and did wonders in
2 proof of his authority. He foretold to Jozadak that he would
3 beget a son who would serve as priest in Jerusalem;[61] he also
congratulated Shealtiel on the birth of a son and gave him the
4 name Zerubbabel. In the time of Cyrus he gave the king a sign

[58] Compare the passage in the Life of Jeremiah, Note 15. Also Wisd. 2 24,
IV Macc 18 8.
[59] Name otherwise unknown.
[60] "Kasdím" the name of the country, Chaldea, as often.
[61] Ezra 3 2.

of victory, and foretold the service which he was destined to perform for Jerusalem, and he praised him greatly.

5 His prophecies uttered in Jerusalem had to do with the end of the nations, with Israel and the temple, with the laziness of
6 prophets and priests, and with a double judgment.[62] After reaching great age he was taken ill, and dying, was buried beside Haggai.

## MALACHI

1 He was born in Sōphā,[63] after the return from the exile.
2 Even in his boyhood he lived a blameless life, and since all the people paid him honor for his piety and his mildness, they called him "Malachi" (angel); he was also fair to look upon.
3 Moreover, whatever things he uttered in prophecy were repeated on that same day by an angel of God who appeared; as had happened in the days when there was no king in Israel, as is written[64] in the book of Judges.[65]
4 While yet in his youth, he was joined to his fathers in his own field.

## NATHAN

1 He, David's prophet, was from Gibeon, of a Hivite clan,[66]
2 and it was he who taught the king the law of the Lord. He foresaw David's sin with Bathsheba, and set out in haste to warn him, but Satan ("Beliar") thwarted his attempt. He found lying by the road the naked body of a man who had been slain;
3 and while he was detained by this duty, he knew that in that
4 night the king had committed the sin; so he turned back to Gibeon in sorrow. Then when David caused the death of Bathsheba's husband,[67] the Lord sent Nathan to convict him.
5 He lived to an advanced old age, and when he died he was buried in his own land.

[62] Zech 9 12.
[63] Name otherwise unknown (cf. possibly I Sam 1 1?).
[64] Judg 2 1–4; 5 23; 6 11–22; 13 3–21.      [65] See Note 62 on the Greek text.
[66] David's prophet and teacher of the law of Moses was a foreigner, see Josh 9 3–27; 11 19.
[67] II Sam 11 6–17.

# AHIJAH

1 He was from Shiloh, the city of Eli, where the tabernacle
2 stood in days of old.[68] He declared of Solomon, that he would
3 provoke the Lord to anger. He also rebuked Jeroboam,[69] because he dealt treacherously with the Lord, and he had a vision
of two bullocks[70] trampling on the people and charging upon the
4 priests. He foretold to Solomon that his wives would bring
disgrace on him and all his house.
5 Upon his death he was buried beside the oak of Shiloh.[71]

## JOED[72]

1 He was of the district of Samarim.[73] He was that prophet
whom the lion attacked and slew, when he had rebuked Jeroboam
2 concerning the bullocks; he who was buried in Bethel beside
the false prophet who led him astray.[74]

## AZARIAH[75]

1 He was from Sūbatha,[76] the prophet who turned away from
2 Judah the captivity that befell Israel.[77] His burial was in his
own field.

[68] Josh 18 1, Judg 18 11.     [69] I Ki 14 7 ff.

[70] I Ki 12 28 f.

[71] See the Life of Hosea, above. There is no mention of this oak of Shiloh
in the Bible.

[72] The name appears in several forms other than those recorded in the Note
on the Greek text, thus Jadai, Jedo, Jadon (Jos. *Antt.* 8, viii, 5) and Iddo
(II Chr 9 29, Targ.). In the last-named passage the Hebrew M. T. has a
double reading, combining Ye'dai and Iddo; while the Greek has the better
tradition, Ιωηδ in the L text, Ιωηλ in Cod. B. The name is doubtless the one
which occurs in Neh 11 7 (where the Grk reads 'Ιωάδ).

[73] Probably southeast of Bethel (Buhl, *Geogr.*, 100, 180), see Josh 18 22,
II Chr 13 4.

[74] I Kings, chap. 13. Syr. adds the name of the false prophet, *Abītōn*.

[75] Son of Oded, II Chr 15 1 ff.

[76] Name otherwise unknown. Perhaps modern Sūbā, a site anciently in-
habited, about eight miles west of Jerusalem (Buhl, *Geogr.*, Note 478). Syr.
*Sqūtha* probably miswriting of Sūbtha.

[77] All texts have the (false) reading: who turned away from Israel the
captivity of Judah. The Heb. text of II Chr 15 3 ff. is in unsatisfactory condi-

## ZECHARIAH SON OF JEHOIADA[78]

1    He was of Jerusalem, the son of Jehoiada the priest, the prophet whom Joash king of Judah slew beside the altar,[79] whose blood the house of David shed within the sanctuary, in the court.[80] The priests buried him beside his father.

2    From that time on there were portentous appearances in the temple, and the priests could see no vision of angels of God, nor give forth oracles from the inner sanctuary; nor were they able to inquire with the ephod, nor to give answer to the people by Urim and Thummim, as in former time.

## ELIJAH

1    He was a Tishbite,[81] from the land of the Arabs,[82] of the family of Aaron, residing in Gilead because Tishbi[83] had been assigned to the priests.

2    At the time of his birth his father, Shobach,[84] saw how certain men of shining white appearance addressed the babe, and that they wrapped him in swaddling clothes of fire and gave him a

3    flame of fire to eat. When he went and reported this in Jerusalem, the oracle gave answer: Fear not; for his dwelling will be light, and his word revelation, and he will judge Israel* with sword and with fire.[85]

---

tion; that which is cryptically referred to is the coming deportation and captivity of the Northern kingdom in various pagan lands ("nation by nation and city by city," vs. 6). Ginzberg, *Legends of the Jews*, VI, 309, gives the gist of these verses quoting from Wayyiqra Rabba 19 9: "And for long seasons Israel will be without the true God."

[78] In the second Epiphanius recension (E1) this biography forms the second half of the biography of Zechariah son of Berechiah! The two Zechariahs are also confused in the present text of Matt 23 35.

[79] The murder referred to in Matt 23 35 and Luke 11 51.

[80] II Chr 24 20–22.

[81] I Ki 17 1; II Ki 1 3, 8.

[82] Transjordania was at this time Arabian (i. e. Nabatean) territory. See the Introduction.

[83] Exact form of the name uncertain, see the Hebrew lexicons.

[84] Compare the name in II Sam 10 16, 18.

[85] MS om.

# ELISHA

1    He was from Abel-meholah,[86] of the territory of Reuben.
2    When he was born, in Gilgal,[87] a marvelous thing happened: the
golden calf bellowed so loudly that the shrill sound was heard
3    in Jerusalem; and the priest announced by Urim and Thummim[88]
that a prophet had been born to Israel who should destroy their
4    graven and molten idols. Upon his death he was buried in
Samaria.

[86] I Ki 19 16.

[87] Gilgal a seat of idol worship, Hos 4 15; 9 15; 12 11, Am 4 5; 5 5. This passage in the Lives is the oldest witness to the belief, found in the writings of certain Church fathers, that one of Jeroboam's two golden calves was set up in Gilgal instead of Dan.

[88] Greek text, $τῶν δήλων$.

# APPENDIX

## Jeremiah and the Reptiles of Egypt

The history of the Greek text of the paragraph dealing with the reptiles of Egypt, and their arch-enemies the serpent-killers, is tangled and obscure; see the notes on the text numbered from 5 to 9. We also encounter in this paragraph strange words, found nowhere else and (hitherto) of quite unknown origin. These puzzles have aroused interest ever since early medieval times, and have produced an amount of curious folklore and of mistaken lexicography.

The famous Alexandrian legend makes Jeremiah perform in Egypt a service like that attributed to Saint Patrick in Ireland and to the warrior-saint 'Uqba ibn Nāfi' at the site of Kairuwān in North Africa, ridding the land of its venomous serpents. Our prophet accomplishes this not only by his prayer but also by introducing into Egypt a snake-destroying creature with a strange name. It has been quite unknown what reptiles called ἐφώθ were exterminated, or what the creatures were which attacked and killed them.

The name of the latter, ἀργόλαι, is given, and their efficiency as ὀφιομάχοι is declared. A Greek gloss, which is found in the oldest known form of the text, adds a learned note on these *argols*, which the prophet (or rather, in the later version, Alexander the Great) "imported from Argos of the Peloponnesus, whence it is that they are called *argolaioi*, that is, 'the beneficent ones from Argos,' for *laios* is regularly used to mean 'of good omen.'" This note, which was taken over into the Greek lexicon of Suidas (tenth century), was widely current.

The origin of this *"argol"* is interesting, and a story of early mistranslation. It is the Greek transliteration of a Hebrew word which is found in Lev 11 22, the only occurrence in the Old Testament. The chapter in Leviticus deals with clean and unclean animals, and verse 22 gives permission to eat grasshoppers, of which four species are named, one of them being the (ḥ)argol. The LXX does not transliterate the four Hebrew nouns, but uses Greek terms, and to one species the name ὀφιομάχης, "snake-fighter," is given. Students of the *Lives* would have paid more attention to this but for two facts: first, locusts do not exterminate snakes; and second, in the LXX of Lev 11 22 the clause containing the interpretation is transposed, so that *another* Hebrew word appears to be the one thus defined.

It is evident that the author of this Jeremiah narrative hands down a folk-tradition which originated and was current in Egypt. The creature which destroyed serpents was of course the ichneumon, and the reason for the astonishing connection with Lev 11 22 can be conjectured, as the result of a popular nickname. In the native Aramaic speech of the Egyptian Jews, this little beast, the ichneumon, or mongoose, was popularly called ḥargolā, "grasshopper," because of its wonderfully quick leaps. The LXX translator of Leviticus, who wrote in Alexandria in the third century B. C., was so familiar with this name that he wrote "snake-fighter," translating the Hebrew *word* (after the manner of the Greek translators), paying no attention to the fact that the context demanded something edible, and particularly a variety of locust.

An interesting contribution is made at this point by another Egyptian scholar, Hesychius of Alexandria, who seems to have lived in the earlier part of the fifth century, though it was only at a later day that his lexicon became well known. His definition of ὀφιομάχος is quoted in the *Lexicon* of Liddell and Scott: "A kind of locust, and the ichneumon." (!) Here the false rendering of the LXX is put side by side with the true interpretation of the unusual Greek word.

The lexicon of Suidas, quoted above, takes another item from our story of Jeremiah. It was inevitable that the harmless creatures, "brought from Argos" to attack and kill the dangerous reptiles, should have been supposed to be *serpents*. Note 8 on the Greek text shows the words τοὺς ὄφεις to be a later insertion, present nevertheless in all the oldest witnesses. It was read there by Suidas, who writes: "᾿Αργόλας, a kind of serpent."

[ 50 ]

Here comes into the later form of the legend the figure of the beneficent snake, and of the *daemon* in serpent form, a subject which would be passed by here without further notice if it were not for one of the secondary versions of the *Lives* which requires to be taken into account, namely the Ethiopic. This version was made from the Greek, very likely in Alexandria, and its text presents this one feature of especial interest, the express designation of the *argols* as serpents of good omen.

The text of the Life of Jeremiah was published from two manuscripts by Johannes Bachmann in his *Aethiopische Lesestücke* (Leipzig, 1893), and is thus very familiar to students of the Ethiopic language. A French translation was made by René Basset in the first instalment of his *Apocryphes Éthiopiens* (Paris, 1893), pages 25–29. Alexander the Macedonian, we are told, brought to the tomb of Jeremiah a kind of serpents which devoured the poisonous ones, and they are called *agātidemānōs* (ἀγαθοὶ δαίμονες).

The present view of this matter is concisely given by W. W. Tarn, article "The Hellenistic Ruler-Cult and the Daemon," *Journal of Hellenistic Studies*, Vol. XLVIII (1928), pages 215 f. He refers to "a legend, probably Jewish, in which Alexander is a snake-master. He had snakes of his own, of a beneficent kind, which he brought to Egypt with him. In one version these succeeded in killing off the poisonous snakes of the country, which were assembled at the tomb of the prophet Jeremiah; in the other version they were unable to manage it until Jeremiah himself lent a hand. These beneficent snakes, called ἀργολαί in one version, are called Agathodaemones in the other." Tarn refers to Suidas, and to the article "Agathodaimon" by Ganschinietz in the Pauly-Wissowa *Supplement* (1918).

The other strange word, ἐφώθ (also νεφωθ, μενεφωθ, μεννεφωθ) has made its own trouble. It is the plural form of the Hebrew noun *'ef'eh*, "viper," a word which passed out of use when the root אפע, in late Hebrew as in Aramaic and Syriac, was supplanted by the root of different origin meaning "hyaena"; thus in Targ. I Sam 13 18 אפעיא means "the hyaenas." (In fact, אפעה, "viper," is an old elative form from the root פעה.) In the popular Aramaic speech of Egypt the word was retained for "viper," necessarily in the Hebrew plural form. It was thus preserved also in Coptic (see below), and in Ethiopic *'af'ōt*, regularly used in translations from the Bible and for either singular or plural.

The native Coptic interpreters of the word seem to have derived their knowledge of it from the *expanded* Greek text of our legend of Jeremiah, and to have guessed at its meaning. Accordingly, we read in Peyron's *Lexicon Linguae Copticae* (1835), ЕФΩΤ, A kind of turtle found in the Nile; and in Crum's *Coptic Dictionary*, "A kind of crocodile." The Semitic origin is completely lost.

In regard to the crocodiles: It is not strange that early attempts should have been made to include these creatures in Jeremiah's work for the Egyptians, and it is only because of the way in which the clauses relating to them are forced into the text, creating unacceptable readings, that the mention of them is recognized (e. g., by Schermann) as a later element. Examination of the two principal versions printed on opposite pages in Nestle's *Marginalien* will now convince the reader. The service rendered by the ichneumon in searching out and devouring the eggs of crocodiles was highly appreciated by the people of Egypt; and it was only in Egypt that were made in our Greek translation of the *Lives* the insertions concerning crocodiles, other water animals, and beneficent snakes.

The brief and unadorned Hebrew Text of this passage delivered in Jerusalem by the Egyptian narrator (see the Introduction) was accepted for the Palestinian work, in spite of the difficulty of imagining locusts which, even with divine help, could drive out the serpents of an infested land.

# TABLE OF CONTENTS